# Stranded Stories from the Operas

## Gerry Zwirn

*Travis & Emery Music*
*17 Cecil Court, London.*

*Stranded Stories from the Operas*

*Gerald Zwirn*

©2010

Published by
Travis & Emery Music Bookshop
17 Cecil Court, London, WC2N 4EZ, United Kingdom.
(+44) 20 7240 2129
neworders@travis-and-emery.com

Hardback: ISBN 978-1-84955-094-9
Paperback: ISBN 978-1-84955-095-6

# Gerry Zwirn

Gerry Zwirn was born in the UK but spent much of his adult life in Italy where he worked as a journalist, writer and technical translator. During this period he was a member of the Foreign Press Club in Rome and covered assignments for British and American publications. He currently resides in South Africa.

He is the founder of the Johannesburg-based Bel Canto Club and gives regular talks on opera. He is also a guest speaker on Classic fm radio and has broadcast on subjects ranging from the operas of Puccini to great singers of the past. His main interest is the operas of Verdi and he is a member of the American Institute for Verdi Studies based in New York. Recently he was invited by the University of Cape Town to present a series of lectures on Verdi operas.

# Stranded Stories from the Operas

A Humorous Synopsis of the Great Operas.

Stranded Stories from the Operas is aimed at the serious opera lover who, in addition to possessing a good knowledge of the subject, has a sense of humour. No author, until now, has dared challenge the esoteric world of opera by relating these stories in a humorous way: opera is far too serious a subject to be made fun of!

Times have changed. In this collection you will find the plots of both The Barber of Seville and The Marriage of Figaro told by Figaro himself in his own inimitable style; Samson and Dalilah and Salome retold in appropriate biblical prose; Shakespearian opera is represented by Othello, Macbeth, Hamlet and Romeo and Juliet while Wagner lovers, after reading Die Meistersinger, Tristan and Isolde and Parsifal, may want to check their Kobbé. What really happened at the Polka saloon that night is told by Nick the barman in Minnie get your gun while Turandot's baffling riddles have been updated to reflect the advances made in education since those ancient times.

Finally, if the reader gets as much pleasure from these stories as the author had in writing them and the illustrator in designing them then the time and trouble spent were well worth the effort.

# Introduction

*Scene: a provincial opera house in Italy. An execrably-sung performance of Cavalleria Rusticana is nearing its long-awaited climax. Alfio and Turiddu, with daggers drawn, stand facing each other, each ready to deliver the fatal thrust. A moment of silence, then...*

*"Hanno ammazzato compare Turiddu!" screams a woman, running onstage.*\*

*"Hanno fatto bene!" shouts a jubilant voice from the gallery.*\*

Humour in opera is of two kinds: intentional and unintentional. Of the former we have, in the comic operas of Rossini, Donizetti, Verdi, Wagner and others, some supreme examples. What of the latter? As the present work endeavours to show, these same composers have provided us with some equally choice examples, albeit unbeknown to themselves or to the vast majority of their audiences.

In the top-C-turvy world of opera, the opera plot has long been an established bogey. Early $19^{th}$-century opera libretti fairly abound in absurdities, and in many cases it is only the music that holds story – and sanity – together. On the other hand, let's admit that one reason why we love opera so much is because of these very absurdities: take them away and much of the magic that makes up opera goes with them. We all know that the enormous soprano who's singing Violetta is not really dying of consumption or that the tenor who's singing Manrico will be freed from his dungeon for a couple of minutes in order to acknowledge the applause following the Miserere.

In this present volume lovers of Italian, French and German opera will be delighted, or otherwise, at finding that their Sacred Cows have, so to speak, been herded into fresh pastures.

Gerrry Zwirn
Bel Canto Club
South Africa


\* *"They have killed neighbour Turiddu!"*
\* *"And a good job too!"*

# Acknowledgements

Extracts from Turandot reproduced by kind permission of:
Universal Music MGB Publications,
via Liguria, 4 – Fraz. Sesto Ulteriano
20098 San Giuliano Milanese MI, Italy

# List of Plots

| | |
|---|---|
| Aïda | 9 |
| The Barber of Seville | 14 |
| Carmen | 19 |
| Cavalleria Rusticana | 25 |
| Così fan tutte | 27 |
| Don Giovanni | 36 |
| L'Elisir d'Amore | 42 |
| Faust | 49 |
| Fidelio | 54 |
| Die Fledermaus | 57 |
| Der Freischütz | 66 |
| The Ballad of La Gioconda | 69 |
| Hamlet | 73 |
| Les Huguenots | 79 |
| Lohengrin | 84 |
| Lubbo M | 88 |
| Macbeth | 92 |
| The Magic Flute | 100 |
| Manon | 105 |
| The Marriage of Figaro | 108 |
| Martha | 113 |
| Die Meistersinger | 117 |
| Mignon | 122 |
| Minnie get your gun | 125 |
| Othello | 129 |
| I Pagliacci | 135 |
| Parsifal | 139 |
| Rigoletto | 143 |
| Romeo and Juliet | 148 |
| Salome | 153 |
| Samson et Dalila | 158 |
| La sonnambula | 162 |
| Tannhäuser | 166 |
| Tosca | 169 |
| La Traviata | 175 |
| Tristan und Isolde | 178 |
| Il trovatore | 182 |
| Turandot | 187 |
| Werther | 192 |
| William Tell | 194 |

# *Aïda*

Opera in 4 acts by Giuseppe Verdi. First produced Cairo 1871

| | |
|---|---|
| Aïda, an Ethiopian slave | soprano |
| Amonasro, king of Ethiopia and Aida's dad | baritone |
| Radames, Egyptian captain of the guard | tenor |
| Pharaoh, king of Egypt | bass |
| Amneris, his daughter, in love with Radames | mezzo |
| Ramfis, High Priest of Egypt | bass |

Priests, priestesses, warriors, messengers, prisoners, populance etc

Scene: Egypt                    Time: Pre-Nasser

*Act 1.*
*Scene 1. The Royal Palace at Memphis.*
A hall flanked by colonnades. High Priest Ramfis, 'Lofty' to his mates, is discussing the military situation with Radames, captain of the guard. The Ethiopians, Lofty tells him, are threatening to invade Egypt, and he drops a hint that Radames may be chosen to lead the Egyptian army against the enemy.

It seems that our hero has fallen for the charms of Aïda, a beautiful Ethiopian slavegirl who acts as Girl Friday to Amneris, daughter of the king. To Radames, Aida is the tops and in the first four words of his opening aria he sings of her heavenly beauty (*Celeste Aïda*) and her hourglass figure (*forma divina):* this last quality is not always evident in performance. Moreover, although Verdi carefully marked the last note of the aria to be sung *pp,* this is interpreted by tenors to mean *painfully piercing* or *powerfully penetrating* but never *pianissimo.*

Amneris now appears, or rather as much of her as the wings will permit. The proud daughter of the Pharoahs and a royal princess to boot, she stands no nonsense from anyone and always gets the last word, as proved at the end of the opera. Amneris is passionately in love with Radames and is sorely peeved her love is not returned. What's more, she suspects there is something between Radames and Aïda but here she's mistaken: owing to the hot sultry Egyptian weather there hasn't even been a *sheet* between them.

To a fanfare of trumpets Pharoah enters. A messenger brings news that the Ethiopians, led by Amonasro, are preparing to attack Egypt south of Suez (cries of *Guerra! Guerra! Guerra!*). Pharoah announces that You-know-who has been chosen as CEO of the Egyptian army (cries of *Ritorna vincitor!*). Poor Aïda finds herself in a no-win situation: love of her country and love for Radames, who will conquer it. What a situation: it's enough to make a mummy cry.

*Scene 2. Interior of the Temple of Vulcan.*
Mysterious chanting from the priestesses is followed by an exotic belly-dance. Radames is brought in and after a brief vulcanisation ceremony what appears to be a silver chamberpot, empty of course, is placed upside down on his head. The scene closes on the words *Immenso Fthà*, which according to Egyptologists means 'Big Brother is watching you'.

Act 2
*Scene 1. Amneris' apartments.*
The curtain rises swiftly to reveal Amneris in her boudoir: too swiftly, as events turn out, because the princess is still getting dressed and is revealed in her flimsy underwear. A right royal row follows between the furious princess and the frightened stage manager. When order has been restored the curtain rises again, accompanied by catcalls and whistles from the delighted audience.

Amneris, now dressed, is seen being dolled up by her handmaidens in readiness for the Big Show. We learn that Radames has been victorious and is returning to a hero's welcome. Aïda enters slowly and sadly, not because of the stage directions but because of a painful corn on her left foot. By tricking her with the false news of Radames' death, Amneris gets Aïda to reveal her love for him. The jealous princess warns Aïda to watch it, for she too loves Radames and being a daughter of the Pharoahs etc ain't standing no nonsense from no one.

*Scene 2. The gates of Thebes.*
The Greatest Show on Earth, operatically speaking, is about to begin. The stage is packed with hundreds of extras dressed as soldiers, standard-bearers, High and Low Priests, warriors, populance etc. In some outdoor productions camels, horses, elephants and other beasts are brought onstage, as well as Amneris.

The famous Grand March is now played. A never-ending stream of victorious soldiers march in slowly from the left, cross the stage and disappear, only to emerge three minutes later again from the left. A favourite game among opera-goers is to pick on one conspicuous member of the chorus and count the number of times he crosses the stage. The present World Record stands at 11 not out (rain stopped play). The stage then fills with more soldiers, chariots, weapons, booty and plunder of war. Finally Radames, seated under a canopy borne by his men, makes his triumphal entry, to the joyful acclaim of the populance.

After hailing Radames as the saviour of his country, the King asks him what he'd like as a reward. Spurning the luxury of a Ferrari G350, a cruise on the QE2 or a week in Manchester our hero asks that the Ethiopian prisoners be brought in. As they enter Aïda rushes excitedly to one of them: it's daddy Amonasro, disguised as an officer. Turning to the King Amonasro pleads for clemency but is immediately howled down by the priests, who demand the death penalty. But Radames, having been given *Carte Blanche* by the King (he already has *Visa* and *Diners Club*) backs up Amonasro's plea and asks that the prisoners be set free. This is strongly opposed by Ramfis but eventually a compromise is reached: the prisoners are allowed to go free but Aïda's dad is kept as surety.

Finally the King turns to Radames and announces that as his reward he will be given the hand of Amneris: the rest of her to follow in weekly instalments. The act closes amid general rejoicing, except again for Aïda who, as in previous scenes, is feeling increasingly marginalized.

*Act 3. The banks of the Nile.*
It is night. This exquisite opening scene, so delicately scored by Verdi for muted violins and violas, and so evocative of a starry, moonlit night, is invariably ruined in performance by either latecomers returning noisily to their seats or by coughing from the already-seated audience. As one cynic remarked, if Egypt's coffers were as full of gold as Covent Garden was as full of coughers, her economy would be in much better shape.

A boat appears, bearing Amneris to the Temple of Isis, but as she steps off she suddenly slips and with a gigantic splash falls into the water. She is quickly rescued by her guards but the incident has put the princess in a right royal temper and she's ready to lash out at the slightest provocation. Needless to say, it's hubby-to-be who gets the brunt of it.

Aïda now enters and sings her famous aria *O patria mia*. She's come to keep a midnight date with Radames but, on hearing footsteps, discovers it's dad instead. Amonasro tells her he is going to war again. He needs to know which route the Egyptian army will take and asks Aida to get this classified info from her lover. When she refuses he hurls her to the ground and denounces her as a slave of the Pharoahs. Her spirit broken she sorrowfully agrees to her father's wishes.

Amonasro goes behind a tree for a quick leak. Radames appears and passionately declares his love but Aïda turns a deaf 'un: save it for Amneris, she tells him. Can't he see they're in a no-win situation? Their only solution is to fly from Egypt, preferably business class. Seeing that Radames remains unconvinced, Aïda conjures up a picture of domestic bliss at the kitchen sink in Ethiopia, and to the tune of *I'll string along with you* he agrees to her plan.

As the two lovers sing of their plans Aïda asks the fatal question about the army's route and Radames replies 'The Napata Gorge'. Amonasro, stepping out from behind the tree, reveals to Radames that not only is he Aïda's dad but also king of Ethiopia. Radames is aghast at having betrayed his country to the enemy but worse is to come: Amneris, who has overheard all, enters and denounces him as a traitor. In another right royal temper she orders the guards to arrest the trio but father and daughter manage to escape. Radames gives himself up to the priests whose vengeance, like the curtain, is about to fall.

*Act 4 Scene 1. A hall in the palace.*
Well, the fat's fairly in the fire. Radames is to be tried in court by Lofty and his mob for having betrayed military secrets to the enemy while Amneris, now feeling remorseful, tries to patch things up with our hero, but to no avail.

The judgement is conducted offstage: this allows the priests to continue their game of poker unseen by the audience. Lofty, who is losing heavily, reads out the treason charge three times, but each time Radames remains silent. Losing patience, as well as $90 on a full house, Lofty announces the terrible verdict: Radames is to be buried alive, with no aircon. Amneris, who's been listening in via a bugging device, hurls such invective against the clergy that whenever *Aïda* is performed in the Eternal City her scene is omitted for fear of offending the Vatican. Radames is led away between guards and the curtain falls.

*Scene 2. The Temple of Vulcan.*
The final scene is divided into two halves. The upper half shows the interior of the temple; the lower half the darkened vault where Radames is condemned to die. In the semi darkness of the vault we can make out a figure standing on the steps: it is Radames, musing on his fate. Suddenly he

hears a sound and Aïda appears. She explains that, learning of the verdict, she had slipped into the vault in advance to share his fate.

Radames takes Aïda into his arms. As the aircon is switched off the two lovers sing their farewell to the world. Amneris appears in the temple above the vault and, as she predicted, gets in the last word, *pace,* before the curtain falls.

# The Barber of Seville

Comic opera in two acts. Music by Gioacchino Rossini.
First produced Rome 1816

| | |
|---|---|
| Figaro, a local barber | baritone |
| Count Almaviva, a local playboy | tenor |
| Dr Bartolo, a local quack | bass |
| Don Basilio, a local music teacher | bass |
| Rosina, a local beauty | mezzo or soprano |
| Scene: Seville | Time: 18$^{th}$ century |

*Act 1 Scene 1. A square in Seville*

¡*"Buenos dias, señor*! I'm going to tell you how I, Figaro, the celebrated barber of Seville, helped Count Almaviva to win the hand, feet and the rest of la bella Rosina.

First of all, señor, before the action begins, there is played this famous overture. Some people say they can actually recognize the character of Figaro weaving its way through the music. Nonsense! the overture has nothing to do with Figaro: maestro Rossini borrowed it from an earlier opera.

It is early morning and dawn is breaking. Why so early, señor, you may ask, to begin an opera? I will tell you: Rossini suffered from insomnia.

Count Almaviva, accompanied by a band of musicians, is about to serenade Rosina, with whom he has fallen madly in love. I should explain, señor, that this Rosina, who is a saucy bag of tricks, is the beautiful and wealthy young ward of old Doctor Bartolo, one of my customers. In order to get his hands on her money, and later on her, he plans to marry her himself, which is why he never lets her out of his sight. Rosina however, is no fool, and has her own ideas about whom she will marry.

The Count sings Rosina a serenade and waits expectantly, but she doesn't appear on her balcony. You know why, amigo? I will tell you: owing to the surrounding darkness, the Count has serenaded the wrong house! He dismisses the musicians with cries of *"basta!'* and then ponders what to do next. And luckily for him and, may I say, for the world of opera, this is where I arrive on the scene. As I'm his ex-valet he quickly puts me in the picture and I promise to help him in his quest: his generous gift of a bag of gold coins had absolutely nothing to do with my decision.

Just then Rosina herself appears on the balcony. What-ta to do? Almaviva, seizing the chance, the moment and a guitar, sings her another serenade in which, under the name of Lindoro, he declares that his love for her is true and his intentions strictly honourable. Can this be the same Count Almaviva we meet in Mozart's opera, you may ask? It is, but although he had been married to Rosina for some years his philandering nature and roving eye remained undimmed.

Hardly has the count finished his second serenade than Rosina suddenly disappears from view. What-ta to do? I have a brilliant idea: in order to gain access to Bartolo's house the Count will disguise himself as a drunken soldier, show the Doctor a billeting order and then elope with Rosina. *Magnifico!* exclaims Almaviva. We congratulate each other on our good fortune and go our separate ways.

*Scene 2. A room in Bartolo's house*

This next scene, señor, introduces us to the Doctor's household and to the saucy Rosina. In the room are chairs, a writing-table, screens and other pieces of furniture. In some productions Rosina is provided with a beautiful pair of tits, which she keeps caged, but on sunny days she likes to dangle them from her balcony, where they attract the admiration of passers-by. We Spaniards, señor, are very fond of birds, and will always find time to admire canaries, budgies or tits.

Rosina has been writing a note to Lindoro, and in her celebrated aria *Una voce poco fa* she tells us what a gentle, loving, docile creature she is. But, she adds, should anyone try to get the better of her, then let him beware, for she can become a spitfire, a viper, a mistress of a hundred snares. As the tempo quickens her coloratura becomes increasing florid and her high notes even higher.

Rosina seals the note and wonders how she can get it to Lindoro without arousing the suspicions of Bartolo, who is awaiting Don Basilio, an unscrupulous rogue and Rosina's music teacher. When he arrives he tells Bartolo that Almaviva has been seen in town and that they must devise a plan. To discredit the Count Basilio suggests a little slandermongering, an art he learned from Ortrud. The two then retire to another room to discuss the marriage contract, leaving the field clear for me.

Entering hurriedly, I ask Rosina for a note to take to Lindoro; can't she write one quickly? With downcast eyes she replies that she cannot: her social position, maidenly modesty, etc forbid her. But after I press her – and believe me, amigo, she has much to press – she agrees. But instead of sitting down to write the note, the cunning little *chica* produces it from her generous bosom – *already written!* What a girl! I depart immediately.

Bartolo returns, full of suspicion as usual, but Rosina foxes him by answering all his questions. In accordance with my plan the Count, disguised as a drunken soldier, enters. He creates a fracas in the room and mispronounces Bartolo's name several times but like everything Almaviva does, he overplays his part and Bartolo, suspecting who he really is, summons the police to arrest him. It is only by revealing his true identity to the officer that he is released. "Bah!" I say to myself, "thanks to Almaviva, back to square one!"

*Act 2 Scene 1. Bartolo's library*

Some hours later. Almaviva, still determined to win Rosina, has devised another ruse: this time he gains access by disguising himself as Don Alonso, a music teacher standing in for Don Basilio who, he tells Bartolo, is ill. When I arrive to shave him the old faggot is so suspicious – suspecting *me*, señor, of all people – that he insists I shave him in the music room where he can keep watch. ¡*Muy bien*! I say to myself as I prepare the lather. Rosina enters and assisted by Don Alonso, begins her music lesson. Although maestro Rossini composed music for this Lesson Scene, the chances are that you will hear instead *Home sweet Home, The last rose of summer, Il Bacio,* Proch's *Air and Variations, Les filles de Cadiz* and, with a little bit of luck, as my friend Mr Doolittle would say, the Mad Scene from *Lucia.*

The lesson over, there is a knock on the door, and -¡*caramba!* – in walks Don Basilio, unwashed, unkempt and very much unwanted. What is worse, señor, is that he is in the best of health and is surprised to find this Don Alonso in his place, of whom he knows nothing. What-ta to do? With my usual quick wit I convince Don Basilio that he has the fever, Rosina adds her concern and a purse of money slipped discreetly into his hand by Almaviva does the rest. This is probably the only instance in opera where a gift of money has the effect of making the receiver *more* ill than before! Basilio is hastily bundled out of the room and we all breathe freely again.

But only for a moment! It's that imbecile of a Count who must clobber things up again. Having reseated himself next to Rosina at the piano, he tells her of our rescue plan and then tries to embrace her – in front of Bartolo! Is the *hombre* mad? Desperately, I try to distract Bartolo's attention by dabbing more lather on his face, but the wily Doctor has seen and heard enough to realise that something's afoot and in a furious rage he orders Almaviva out of the house. "Bah!" I say to myself for a second time that day, "this Almaviva was always such a silly Count!".

*Scene 2. Doctor Bartolo's room*

And so, amigo, we come to the last scene in this Spanish *olla podrida.* Having smelt a rat, ie Almavivia, Bartolo decides to take the Spanish bull by the horns: he tells Basilio to fetch a notary so that he and Rosina can be married immediately. He then convinces Rosina, by means of the note she sent Almaviva, that the Count has been deceiving her: Lindoro is merely the Count's servant, employed by Almaviva to gain her affections. Out of pique she agrees to marry Bartolo at once and discloses to him our plan to rescue her that night. The Doctor hurries off to alert the nightwatch.

A few hours later. A storm is brewing but Almaviva and I succeed in getting onto Rosina's balcony. She appears and accuses Lindoro of being faithless and deceitful. Although she's absolutely right, she only finds that out in Mozart's opera. At this moment Almaviva reveals that he and Lindoro are one and the same person: the deception, he tells her, was only to prove her love for him. As the Beatles were to sing later, *Yeah, yeah, yeah*.

We return to the balcony to make our escape but ¡*caramba!* the ladder has disappeared. What-ta to do? Fortunately at that moment Basilio returns with the notary. Since it is merely a matter of substituting bridegrooms the marriage ceremony is performed on the spot, helped by the Count placing a pistol at Basilio's head, and the happy couple are finally united. Doctor Bartolo arrives with the watch but as it was running a few minutes slow he is too late and has to wait for Mozart's opera before he gets a wife.

And so, amigo, from me thanks for listening and ¡*hasta la vista!*"

# Carmen

Opera in 4 acts. Music by Georges Bizet.
First produced Paris 1875

| | |
|---|---|
| Carmen, a Spanish gypsy | mezzo-soprano |
| Dee Jay, a corporal | tenor |
| Eskimo, a bullfighter | baritone |
| Micki, a village maiden | soprano |
| Mercedes )<br>Benz      ) gypsy friends of Carmen | sopranos |
| Zuniga, an army officer | bass |

Soldiers, smugglers, street-vendors etc.

Scene:  Seville                                                    Time: 1820s

*Act 1. A square in Seville*

It is mid-morning and the busy square is full of people going about their daily task, viz idling. Small groups of bored soldiers, loafing about in their guardroom, watch the idling crowd and ogle the women. A local barber enters and is just about to launch into *Largo al factotum* when the horrified prompter tells him he's in the wrong opera. The barber withdraws hastily. The people laugh and continue with their daily task.

Micki, a cute little blonde with hair in plaits and a blue miniskirt, enters shyly and the boredom of the soldiers quickly vanishes. Approaching them timidly, she explains she is looking for a corporal with the impossible name of Don José Lizzarrabengoa, or Dee Jay to his mates.  He'll be serving shortly, they tell her: in the meantime, they assure the audience with a wink, they'll be delighted to serve *her*: all she has to do is join them in the guardroom. Politely declining their invitation, Micki leaves and the soldiers resume their idle sport of watching the idle populace idling.

A group of soldiers, led by Dee Jay and Zuniga, marches in, and the Changing of the Guard takes place.  This is an old Spanish custom allowing soldiers who have been on guard duty to be relieved, which they do behind the barrack wall.  When they depart the new guards take over their duties, viz  watching the crowd and ogling the women.

Another old custom now takes place, much to the delight of the male population. As a bell tolls midday men swarm into the square to get a closer squiz of the cigarette-girls as they emerge from the tobacco factory for their smoke-break. It's exceptionally hot inside the factory and as there's no aircon the girls strip down to the bare essentials for comfort. Strolling about the square they provocatively wiggle their hips as they puff at their cigarettes, blowing the smoke upwards in time to the music and enjoying the attention of the men. As required by law each girl carries a government health warning.

It's now time for the entrance of the *protagonista*. At a sign from the prompter some of the men cry out that they don't see *la Carmencita,* but before you can say Speedy Gonzales she suddenly appears, wearing a short red skirt, a flower in her mouth and precious little else. Darting across the stage, she approaches the men and sings the habanera, better known to the ignorant as the 'Have-a-banana' from *Carmen.*

Catching sight of Dee Jay Carmen strolls over to him and insolently asks what he's doing. To his innocent reply that he's fixing his priming-iron she bursts into peals of laughter. She then takes a cassia flower from her corsage and throws it in his face before returning to the factory with the other girls. Dee Jay picks up the flower and after inhaling its perfume puts it carefully into his pocket: the magic is already working.

As the crowds disperse Micki reappears. She brings a letter and a smacker from Dee Jay's mother, both of which she promptly delivers. As Micki leaves, our hero vows he will marry her but just then a tremendous hubbub breaks out from inside the factory and the girls come streaming out in much excitement. Yes, you've guessed it: it's that's gypsy again. This time she's stabbed a fellow worker during a heated trade union dispute and Zuniga, after hearing the evidence, sentences her to prison. Tying her hands, he orders Dee Jay to escort her to the local clink.

The stunning gypsy, who knows a thing or three about men, now turns her charms upon the young corporal. In a seductive seguidilla she sings of a tavern-cum-bordello called Lillas Pasta where, she tells Dee Jay meaningly, they'll soon be dancin', drinkin' and lovin' together if he'll let her free. Intoxicated by her charms, our hero eagerly agrees and lets her escape while en route to prison, to the vast amusement of the populance.

*Act 2. Chez Lillas Pastia*

A month later. The curtain goes up to reveal Carmen and her gypsy friends dancing for Zuniga and other army officers. Zuniga, who now fancies Carmen strongly, tells her that Dee Jay, who was imprisoned and demoted for letting her escape, has been freed that day. With a wink at the audience Carmen remarks that while Dee Jay may have lost his corporal's stripes at least he still has his privates.

The scene is now set for the grand entry of Eskimo, the celebrated bullfighter, the 'Glory of Granada'. According to his press agent Eskimo's skill is such that he can hit a bull at 100 metres with his eyes closed; as a result, he is reputed to be the biggest bulls-hitter in the business. Accompanied by an entourage of PR men, gofers and hangers-on, he makes his triumphal entrance.

After acknowledging the applause from the claque, whom his agent paid in advance, he raises his glass, his arm and his voice and bursts into the Toreador Song, in which he is enthusiastically joined by the chorus, who this way hope to get free tickets for his next *corrida*.

By this time our intrepid bullfighter, deeply smitten by the well-displayed charms of the bewitching gypsy, starts to chat her up, but although Carmen is impressed by his prowess over wine, women and bull, her thoughts are with her soldier and she tells him that there's nothin' doin' – at least not in this act. Knowing his chance will come in act 3, Eskimo goes off with his crowd of hangers-on, singing all the way.

Next to appear are two comedians, disguised as smugglers, whose plan is to smuggle pot from Morocco via Gib. They ask the three gypsy girls for help but Carmen refuses: she is *amoureuse,* she tells them, so head over heels in love that she no longer knows whether she's Carmen or going. As they argue, a voice is heard approaching: it is Dee Jay, singing an unaccompanied air horribly out of tune. Unable to bear it, the others quickly hide, leaving Carmen to meet her lover alone.

Dee Jay, full of confidence, breezes in. After embracing Carmen he takes off his sabre and swordbelt: after a month in clink he's evidently eager to get down to the rest of the bargain. Carmen, assisted by a castanets-player concealed under the stage, now sings and dances, watched rapturously by her new lover. But just then a bugle is heard, sounding the retreat, and Dee Jay, getting to his feet, prepares to leave.

"Where the !!!***!!!***!!!***!!!***!!! are you going?" demands Carmen angrily. *"Barracks!"* comes the hurried reply. "And you!" she hurls back at him, together with his sabre and swordbelt. Taking the flower from his tunic pocket Dee Jay sings the impassioned Flower Song, in which he begins by cursing the day he met Carmen and ends by cursing Bizet for writing a well-nigh impossible *pianissimo* high B flat at the end.

In an equally impassioned plea, Carmen urges Dee Jay to take her away on his horse to the mountains: this proves somewhat difficult, seeing that he came on foot. A sudden loud knock on the door interrupts their squabbling and Zuniga enters. Expecting to find Carmen alone he curtly dismisses Dee

Jay, but our hero ain't having none of it and drawing his sword challenges Zuniga to a duel. Carmen hurriedly calls in the smugglers and Zuniga is disarmed. Having raised his sword against a superior officer our hero is for the high jump but, rather than go AWOL, he throws in his lot with Carmen and the Gipoes. The act closes with a rousing finale in praise of *liberté, egalité et fraternité*.

*Act 3. The smugglers' mountain hideout*

The scene reveals smugglers busy carrying bales of duty-frees smuggled out of Gib. It seems that relations between Carmen and Dee Jay have soured and they're no longer on speaks. Carmen joins Mercedes and Benz who are reading their fortunes at cards. Mercedes, who seeks riches, turns up diamonds; Benz, who craves love, turns up hearts; Carmen, who is after the jackpot, turns up spades. The smugglers leave with their goods and Dee Jay, armed with a carbine, is left to guard the camp.

Micki enters. How she found her way to such a secret hideout is known only to the producer. She brings another message from mum but hearing a shot she quickly hides behind a rock, presumably to answer an urgent call of Nature. The shot was fired by Dee Jay at Eskimo the bullfighter, who has come to find his gypsy gal. A fight with knives ensues and Eskimo is rescued just in the nick of time. He thanks Carmen for saving his life and hands out comps to the chorus for his upcoming *corrida* in Seville.

Just then one of the smugglers drags in Micki, found hiding behind a rock. She tells Dee Jay that mum is asking for him but he refuses to go; but when he learns mum is dying he agrees. As he and Micki prepare to leave Eskimo's song about the bulls comes floating up from below and Carmen's hand steals to her bosom in anticipated delight. Dee Jay, with a menacing gesture, warns her to stay away and the act closes.

*Act 4. Outside the bullring*

It's the big day and all Seville has flocked to see the great Eskimo perform his prodigious bulls-hitting feat. As the crowd arrives excitement mounts: ticket-touts report record business while outside the bullring program-sellers, fruit-sellers and pita-sellers hawk their wares on the excited crowd. After a magnificent procession Eskimo and Carmen appear, each dressed to kill, but for different reasons. In a brief duet (*See to Mame*) they declare their love. Carmen remains outside the bullring for the coming showdown with Dee Jay, of whose presence she has already been warned.

Dee Jay emerges. His clothes are in rags, his swagger has gone and having pawned his braces he has difficulty in keeping his trousers up. He is also scruffy and unshaven, Figaro and other local barbers having shut up shop to attend the bullfight.

He begins by pleading with Carmen to return, but she merely titters at his tatters and ignores him (loud cries of ¡olé! from the bullring). His pleading increases but Carmen remains unmoved (louder cries of ¡¡olé!! from the bullring). His temper almost at breaking point, Dee Jay pleads for the last time (he's become a pleading nuisance) but Carmen tells him bluntly that all is over between them and that she will never return, even at the cost of her own life (deafening cries of ¡¡¡olé!!! from the bullring).

By this time, what with all the yelling from inside the arena and the mounting excitement outside, communication has become difficult and Carmen, cellphone in hand, returns Dee Jay's ring to make him understand, once and for all, that *tout est fini, mais oui*. His reason gone, Dee Jay pulls out a knife but Carmen, never one to show fear, makes a dash for the gates. Dee Jay follows her and stabs her to death, at the very moment Eskimo is proclaimed victor. Dee Jay throws himself upon her lifeless body and the curtain comes down for the last time.

.

# Cavalleria Rusticana

Opera in one act. Music by Pietro Mascagni.
First produced Rome 1890

| | |
|---|---|
| Santuzza, a village maiden | soprano |
| Turiddu, a soldier | tenor |
| Alfio, a waggoner | baritone |
| Lola, wife to Alfio | mezzo |
| Mamma Lucia, Turiddu's mum | mezzo |

Scene: Sicily                                    Time: late 19$^{th}$ century

The opera begins with an orchestral prelude. Halfway through it's suddenly interrupted by the tenor (who else?) who at this moment decides he'd like to *riscaldare la voce* by singing a Sicilian song behind the curtain, leaving the conductor fuming.

It's Easter morning. As the bells chime the villagers cross the street, the square and themselves before entering the church. A few moments later an agitated Santuzza enters and for good reason. Yes, you've guessed it: someone has left a bun in the oven and it wasn't the baker. Catching sight of Mamma Lucia she asks where Turiddu is, but before old Lucia can reply a cracking of whips is heard and Alfio enters. He is Lola's husband, which is why he carries a whip. In a rousing aria Alfio sings about himself and his horse, interspersed with louder crackings of whips. By this time the poor horse becomes so frightened that he gives his opinion of his *padrone* in no uncertain manner. Two cursing stagehands are called in to clear up the mess.

Santuzza now tells Mamma Lucia her sad story. Before Turiddu became a soldier he and Lola were lovers. On his return from the wars he found that Lola had married Alfio. Although he's since taken up with Santuzza he still strongly fancies la Lola, who has obviously got what Santuzza hasn't. Old Lucia feigns surprise at this news and enters the church, leaving Santuzza to have it out with her son.

Turiddu swaggers in a moment later, and the unhappy Santuzza immediately accuses him of deserting her in her hour of need and of shacking up with Lola. Turiddu hotly denies this, saying that he was visiting his mate Franco Forte, who runs a wineshop in the next village, but Santuzza tells him he's been seen near Lola's house. Their conversation is interrupted by the entrance of la Lola who saunters sexily across the stage and into church, watched by Turiddu with hungry eyes.

Seeing the effect la Lola has on her lover, Santuzza pleads with him to stay with her, but he refuses. With a violent push he throws her to the ground and follows la Lola. The desperate Santuzza curses him with the savage cry of 'A te, la male Pasqua!' as she swears vengeance on her faithless lover for putting her in the pudding club.

And this being a one-acter, she doesn't have long to wait. Alfio enters and Santuzza, mad with jealousy, 'reveals all', as the tabloids like to proclaim. Alfio is in such a fearful temper that he forgets to crack his whip. Santuzza, frightened by the trouble she has wrought by opening her big mouth, leaves. The stage is left empty while the orchestra plays the famous intermezzo, this time without interruption from the tenor.

The service over, Turiddu invites the villagers to his mother's wineshop for drinks on the house. Holding up a glass of red wine, he breaks out into a lively brindisi; when he sees Alfio, he breaks out into a cold sweat. Like Escamillo facing the bull, he senses that the Moment of Truth has come. The two men sullenly eye each other; then Turiddu goes up to Alfio and in his nervousness half-bites off Alfio's right ear. The two men then agree to settle their differences *alla siciliana*. Alfio leaves.

Turiddu, his swagger gone, embraces Mamma Lucia. In a passionate farewell he tells her that should anything happen to him she should blame Santuzza who, thanks to her big mouth, started it all. He then rushes off to meet Alfio. The duel is to take place offstage, in accordance with the Trade Union regulation "One man, one mess", which forbids members to clean up a second mess in the same opera.

Mamma Lucia, bewildered by all the comings and goings, remains on stage. Santuzza hurries in and tries to comfort her. There is a moment of silence, and then a woman's voice shrieking out: "Neighbour Turiddu has been killed!": his life, like the opera, is over.

# Così fan tutte

Comic opera in two acts by Mozart.
First produced Vienna 1790

| | |
|---|---|
| Fiordiligi ) two | soprano |
| Dorabella ) sisters | mezzo |
| Despina, their maid | soprano |
| Ferrando, an officer | tenor |
| Guglielmo, his friend | baritone |
| Don Alfonso, an elderly bachelor | bass-baritone |

Scene: Naples                    Time: $18^{th}$ century

*Act 1. Scene 1. A café in Naples.*
Two young officers boast their sweethearts are forever faithful. Their cynical friend, Don Alfonso, wagers their respective lovers are no more faithful than other women.

| | |
|---|---|
| Ferrando | I am prepared thy bet to take<br>to prove my lover's true<br>my Dorabella is no fake<br>deceive she'd never do |
| Gug | The same doth go for my sweetheart<br>Fiordiligi is her name<br>her love for me will never part<br>she'd rather die of shame! |
| Don Al | One hundred scudi I hereby<br>do offer as reward<br>"Terms and conditions do apply"<br>we'll see who best has scored!<br>It's time to start your wooing, mates<br>with honeyed words and love-rhyme<br>so buckle up, put on yer skates<br>we're running out of real-time! |
| All | So be it! Done! now for some fun<br>let's see what's to discover<br>we'll first drop by to say 'Goodbye'<br>then re-appear as lovers! |

*Scene 2. A garden by the sea. Dorabella and Fiordiligi gaze rapturously at their lovers' portraits encased in miniatures they are wearing.*

Dora               How handsome my Ferrando is
                         how dashing and so knightly
                         and very soon shall I be his
                         in marriage vows made rightly

Fior                O sister, dear, I seem to hear
                         the sound of steps approaching *[opens door]*
                         it's Don Alfonso! welcome here!
                         of course you're not encroaching!

Don Al           A thousand pardons, I thee pray
                         but there's no time to lose,
                         the TV channel said today
                         "Here is the Breaking News:
                         the regiment that's stationed here
                         is ordered off to war"
                         so be prepared to weep, my dear
                         I hear the cannons roar!

Dora and Fior   O woe is me! this cannot be!
                         our happiness is blighted
                         the end is nigh, I want to die
                         shall we be e'er united?

*Ferrando and Guglielmo enter and bid a sorrowful farewell to their sweethearts.*
                         The drumbeats echo down the street
                         we cannot shirk our duty
                         we hear the sound of marching feet
                         the band plays loud and *tutti!*
                         The ship's now waiting to depart
                         it's ready to weigh anchor
                         I feel your wildly beating heart
                         farewell, my love, no rancour! *[they embark]*

*Scene 3. A room in the sisters' house. They continue moping at the loss of their lovers.*

Dora               Our men have gone off to the war
                         and left us brokenhearted
                         it really makes us feel so sore
                         to know that they've departed

Fior    The moment that they said 'goodbye'
       I felt my heart was broken
       my only wish is now to die
       how I adore this token *[looks at miniature]*

Despina   O ladies, will you listen, please
       and cease your endless pining
       just get up from your hands and knees
       it looks as if you're dying!
       Your men are fighting for our King
       so stop your tears and sighing
       and in the meantime have a fling
       it's much more fun than crying!

*Despina, bribed by Don Alfonso, admits Ferrando and Guglielmo into the house disguised as rich Albanians. As part of Don Alfonso's plan they try making love to each other's fiancées but find that their advances are indignantly repulsed.*

Fior *[to Despina]* How dare you let into the house
       these men, these total strangers?
       their lewd advances we shall douse
       amid such lurking dangers!

*Don Alfonso, who has been watching events while concealed, enters. On seeing the two Albanians he pretends they are his greatest friends and greets them warmly.*

       Dear ladies, may I introduce
       my friends from Eastern clime
       for trivia they have no use
       in culture they're sublime!

*The two sisters are reassured but Fiordiligi proclaims her fidelity. They then enter an adjoining garden. Suddenly, voices are raised in alarm: the two Albanians, thwarted in their amorous intentions, each produce a phial of poison which they now swallow.*

Both     Farewell, dear friends, the end is nigh
       farewell, my turtle-dove
       with these last words I fain would die
       of unrequited love!
*[they fall to the ground,' 'writhing' in agony]*

Fior and Dora Oh saints above! what have we done?
       we've brought this trouble on
       Despina, quickly rescue us
       and help them ere they're gone!

*Despina disappears and returns disguised as a doctor. Producing an enormous magnet she passes an 'electric current' through the bodies of the two Albanians and 'restores' them back to life. Thinking they are now in Heaven they mistake the two sisters for goddesses.*

| | |
|---|---|
| Both | Sweet goddesses, we ask no more
we surely are in heaven
no longer stand we at Death's door
instead we're on Cloud Seven!
To celebrate our right near miss
and help us to endure
oh won't you give us one small kiss
just to complete the cure! |
| Dora & Fior *[angrily]* | Begone from here, we have no need
to enter in flirtations
and furthermore we take no heed
of worthless protestations!
So get thee gone, thy presence here
won't change the situation
we trust we've made our feelings clear
so  no more adulation! |

*Act 2. Scene 1. Despina's boudoir.*
Despina *[alone]* The purpose of my little plan
     is make them feel a woman
     ensure that each one gets her man
     and teach them to be human
     it seems to me that soon I'll see
     my ladies getting keener
     I can't afford to have them bored
     not if my name's Despina!

*Scene 2. A room. The two sisters are discussing what to do.*
Dora    Despina's right, we're too upright
     why not enjoy temptation
     my spirits soar, no more a bore
     I feel such palpitation
     I rather like the dark-haired one
     his voice is soft and gentle *[aside]*
     my heart you have already won
     you sexy Oriental!

| | |
|---|---|
| Fior | I long to meet that man again<br>I find him truly hunky<br>losing him would cause me pain<br>he's kinda cool and funky! |
| Both | So let's enjoy this harmless flirt<br>which love its passion fanned<br>who knows what Fate will now assert *[aside]*<br>perhaps a one-night stand! |

*Scene 3. A garden by the sea. On a barge, decorated with flowers, the two Albanians accompanied by the small orchestra on board, sing a welcome to the two sisters.*

> This serenade to you we sing
> two sisters we adore
> it really is a charming thing
> young Mozart wrote the score!

*Scene 4. A garden. Ferrando and Guglielmo resume their courting of each other's fiancée.*

| | |
|---|---|
| Gug | O come, beloved, let us walk<br>this lover's path together<br>as we're alone we need not not talk<br>of idle things or weather *[they embrace]* |
| Dora | For me thou art the only one<br>I find your words so tender<br>Beloved, thou my heart hath won<br>I totally surrender! |

*The two Albanians meet in the garden and compare notes. Ferrando tells Guglielmo that Fiordiligi has not yielded to his ardent wooing. Guglielmo, on the other hand, reports that Dorabella is now virtually his and that Ferrando has lost his wager.*

| | |
|---|---|
| Ferr | I've been betrayed, I feel dismayed<br>I see it now too clearly<br>of me a fool's been truly made<br>this wager's cost me dearly! |
| Don Alfonso | No need to fret, you'll win your bet<br>and Fiordiligi's honour<br>you're not done yet, discharge your debt<br>you'll get this prima donna! |

*Scene 5. In the house the two sisters discuss the day's events with Despina.*

Dora    What is it that doth throb inside
        my breast, and makes me tingle?
        'Tis love, I know, for with one blow
        he made my poor heart jingle!

Fior     I have a plan, how my heart warms!
        a plan I mean to follow
        Despina! bring us uniforms
        which we shall don tomorrow

        And there upon the battlefield
        we'll find our faithful lovers
        and be united, or be killed
        let's see what Fate uncovers!

*Meanwhile, Ferrando and Guglielmo have been listening from another room. Ferrando rushes in and with outstretched arms addresses Fiordiligi.*
        I beg of you, my darling treasure
        do not venture on this trip
        stay with me, be mine forever
        of Love's nectar we shall sip
        Here we two can live at leisure
        offer me thy rosy lip
        we'll enjoy a life of pleasure
        so do not abandon ship!

*Unable to resist Ferrando's passionate outburst she falls rapturously into his waiting arms.*

Gug     What a change in fortune hits me
        I can scarce believe my eyes!
        Oh how could you, Fiordiligi
        trick me with such blatant lies?
        I did mock Ferrando wrongly
        when we in the garden met
        now the tables turned upon me
        and it's I who'll lose the bet!

Don Al    List to me, pray do not tarry
        carry out what I proclaim
        these two girls you now shall marry
        and so end our little game!

*Scene 6. A brightly lit salon prepared for a wedding feast. Despina disappears and returns disguised as a notary.*

| | |
|---|---|
| Despina | The wedding contract's now been readied<br>all you have to do is sign<br>whereupon you four are wedded<br>just sign on the dotted line! |

*All four sign. Suddenly the sound of a military band is heard approaching: Ferrando and Guglielmo have returned. The horrified sisters quickly bundle the two Albanians into an adjoining room. A few moments later they appear dressed in their officers' uniforms.*

| | |
|---|---|
| Ferr & Gug | Here we are, our dearest treasures<br>safe returned from war's alarms<br>let's rejoice and sing gay measures<br>your reward: our loving arms! |

*Suddenly they see the wedding contract which Don Alfonso has carefully thrown down. Enraged, they go off in hot pursuit of the two Albanians. A few moments later they re-enter, dressed in their Albanian costumes and confront the two terrified women.*

| | |
|---|---|
| Ferr & Gug | Yes, once again we've been betrayed<br>you women can't be trusted<br>whatever plans you may have laid<br>we surely now have busted! |
| Dora & Fior | O dearest loves, forgive us do<br>we meant no harm by flirting<br>we'd ne'er deceive you, that is true<br>our consciences are hurting!<br>What started as a harmless game<br>was naught but a distraction<br>we're not to blame for what became<br>a "Non-stop Super Action!" |
| Don Al | No need to pine, the trick was mine<br>the game was all my doing<br>I made a bet I won't regret<br>to prove how fraught is wooing!<br>Now let's forgive and start to live<br>a life that's full of riches<br>be not deterred by what you've heard<br>just overcome the glitches! |

All *[happily]*   And so we reach the joyous end
 our couples reunited
 their saddened hearts are on the mend
 for all the wrongs are righted
 These closing bars from Mozart's nib
 reflect such timeless beauty
 let's drink a toast to Women's Lib
 because *Così fan tutte!*

                  **CURTAIN**

# Don Giovanni

Opera in 2 acts by Mozart.
First produced Prague 1787.

| | |
|---|---|
| Don Giovanni, a sex-mad cad | baritone |
| Leporello, his dumb servant | bass |
| The Commendatore, a Spanish nobleman | bass |
| Donna Anna, his frumpy daughter | soprano |
| Don Ottavio, her fatuous lover | tenor |
| Donna Elvira, a lovelorn lady | soprano |
| Zerlina, a comely wench | soprano |
| Masetto, her nerdy fiancé | tenor |

Scene: Seville                                  Time: 17$^{th}$ century

*Act 1. Scene 1. It is night. Don Giovanni has secretly gained access to Donna Anna's apartments in an attempt to seduce her. Leporello, waiting outside, bemoans his fate.*

Lep        This life is not for you, ol' Leporello
               before you met the Don you were a fellow
               renowned for wit, and never one for bragging
               now all you do is gripe while Master's shagging!

*[The Don, his face concealed by a cloak, rushes out of the house, pursued by Anna.]*

Anna      Begone, o vile seducer, from this palace
               thy presence here hath filled me deep with malice
               I know thy smoochy voice, thy artful manner
               'twill never be forgot by Donna Anna!

*[The Commendatore, alerted by the fracas, challenges the Don to a duel but is mortally wounded. The Don and Leporello flee the scene. Donna Anna is distraught].*

| | |
|---|---|
| Anna | O horrid sight, my father's now a goner |
| | unjustly slain for saving daughter's honour |
| *[to Don Ottavio]* | |
| | avenge this monstrous crime, thy contribution |
| | will be to bring this fiend his retribution |

*Scene 2. A street in Seville. Donna Elvira, jilted by Don Giovanni, laments her destiny. Leporello attempts to console her by reading the list of the Don's conquests.*

| | |
|---|---|
| Lep | Look here, madame, this book's about the Don |
| | it lists the girls whose virtue now is gone |
| | his conquests of the female population |
| | reveal his love for instant copulation! |

*Elvira, shocked at these revelations, goes sadly away, watched by Leporello.*

| | |
|---|---|
| Lep | The way my master treats his dames is shocking |
| | his only thought is where's the next for bonking! |

*Scene 3. Peasants are celebrating the wedding of Masetto and Zerlina. Don Giovanni, having seen Zerlina, tells Leporello to lead Masetto away so that he can seduce her.*

Don G *[to Zerlina]*
        Just come with me, my dear, but make it snappy
        I've something really cool to make you happy *[aside]*
        These buxom peasant girls are chaste and humble
        I'll quickly chat her up before we tumble!

*Zerlina, flattered by the Don's attentions, follows him to his palace. As they are about to enter Donna Elvira suddenly appears.*

| | |
|---|---|
| Elvira | Hold on a moment, Don, not quite so fast |
| | this escapade you've planned may be your last |
| | Zerlina, yield thee not to his temptation |
| | his only wish with you is fornication! |
| | |
| Don G | The poor soul is demented, has no tact |
| | she's truly gone ballistic, that's a fact |
| | ignore her foolish talk, she is quite scatty |
| | next thing she'll claim she's Adelina Patti! |

*[addressing the peasants]*
        Dear friends, come join me at my house of leisure
        there's lots to eat and drink and fruits of pleasure
        and dear Zerlina, love is in the offing
        let's slip upstairs while all are busy scoffing!

*Scene 4. The Don's garden. Enter Anna, Elvira and Ottavio heavily masked.*
Anna            At last the evil villain's in our power
                 to capture him we must within the hour
                 his lavish party therefore we'll attend
                 and bring his retribution in the end!

*Scene 5. The ballroom. The three masked figures are made welcome by the Don.*
Don G           O welcome, gentle maskers, to the ball
                 my humble home is open to you all
                 a minuet is starting just by chance
                 so prithee take your partner for the dance
                 The local band will play a cool fandango
                 another on the stage will play a tango
                 and if it's hotter action that you're after
                 just ask the band to play the new Lambada!

*Leporello leads Masetto away as the Don entices Zerlina into an adjoining room. Suddenly her scream for help is heard. Pretending that Leporello is the culprit the Don holds him at swordpoint.*
Don G           Behold the wretch that tried to snatch Zerlina
                 I caught him in the act, the base deceiver
                 to think this rascal trick'd me into making
                 him servant in my house; he's yours for taking!

*The guests gather round Zerlina. Don Ottavio unsheathes his sword.*
Ottavio           'Tis useless, Don Giovanni, to deceive us
                 we see through thy disguise, so do believe us
                 surrender thou thy sword, renounce ambition
                 thy evil soul is destined for perdition!

*The Don, sword in hand, fights them off and makes his escape as the curtain falls.*

*Act 2. Scene 1. A square outside Elvira's house. The Don, who is planning to seduce Elvira's maid, exchanges hat and cloak with Leporello and in this disguise awaits events.*
Lep *[aside]*     My master's off again on his adventures
                 I'd better wash me face and brush me dentures
                 this time Elvira's maid's the one he's wooing
                 with his technique in minutes they'll be screwing!

*Donna Elvira appears on her balcony. Mistaking the disguised Leporello for her former lover she entreats him to return. The Don, hidden from view, speaks to her in loving tones.*

Don G          "Come to my arms, Elvira mine
                   no more shall we be parted
                   our loving hearts do now entwine
                   which Cupid swiftly darted"

*Deceived by the Don's words, Elvira rushes down into the street and addresses the disguised Leporello in equally loving words, much to his amusement. When they depart, the Don sings a serenade to her maid.*

Don G          In penance do I hereby kneel
                   and humbly beg thy pardon
                   thy virtue I have come to steal
                   so meet me in the garden!
                   I'll first prepare some tasty fare
                   to stoke up hidden fires
                   a drink or two will see us through
                   and waken our desires!

*Scene 2. A courtyard outside Donna Anna's house. Elvira continues to address 'the Don' with words of love but Leporello is getting fed up and plans to escape.*

Lep *[aside]*     I've really had enough by now
                   of amorous attentions
                   her honeyed words no longer wow
                   nor passionate intentions
                   now in a mo I'll have my say
                   and disappear to stump her
                   then swifty plan my getaway
                   by which time I'd have dumped her!

*Leporello escapes but is captured by Anna and Ottavio, who mistake him for the Don.*

Anna           Rejoice, dear friends, success is surely crowned
                   the evil Don Giovanni has been found
                   this time he won't escape from our detention
                   let's kill him now, we've no need for pretension!

*Leporello removes his disguise and reveals he's not the Don. He is allowed to escape.*

*Scene 3. A cemetery. In the background a statue of the Commendatore. As the Don relates the day's events to Leporello a mysterious voice calls him from the statue.*

| | |
|---|---|
| Comm | Repent, o evil-doer, heed my warning |
| | else death will surely claim thee before morning! |
| | |
| Lep | I beg thee, master, do not take this lightly |
| | for Fate tonight will strike in mode unsightly |
| | this eerie statue that doth speak so brightly |
| | addresses thee in accents bold and mighty! |
| | |
| Don G | What nonsense this!  If I'm indeed a sinner |
| [to Leporello] | kindly invite the old buffoon to dinner! |
| | |
| Lep | O gentle statue, pray you, do not scupper |
| | this bold request to join *padron* for supper |
| | the music played tonight will make you high |
| | you'll hear young Mozart's hit  called *'Non piu andrai!'* |

*The statue nods its head in assent. Leporello is terrified but the Don remains calm.*

*Scene 4. Dining room of the Don's palace.  The Don is enjoying a fine dinner. Having forgotten to sing his 'Champagne aria' in act 1 he opens a bottle and sings it now.*

| | |
|---|---|
| Don G | This bottle rare of Bollinger is precious |
| | James Bond himself would certainly be jealous |
| | a glass I'll offer to Commendatore |
| | it hopefully recalls his days of glory! |

*Donna Elvira,  bursting into the room, begs the Don to give up his wicked ways but he scornfully rejects her entreaties.*
| | |
|---|---|
| Don G | Begone, o foolish woman from my presence |
| | thy crazy rantings bore me to the essence |
| | for I am Don Giovanni, prince of charmers |
| | my fame has even reached the far Bahamas! |

*As Elvira leaves she emits a frightened scream. Leporello runs to investigate and returns shaking with fear: at the door is the statue of the Commendatore waiting to be admitted!*

| | |
|---|---|
| Comm | I've come in answer to thy invitation |
| | thy offer here to sup was no temptation |
| | if thou willst not repent of thy past action |
| | then payback time shall be my satisfaction! |

*He offers his hand to the Don who grasps its icy coldness. The Don finds his strength leaving him but even as the icy grip increases he refuses to repent.*
Comm   Don't mess with me, thou unrepentant knave
       my task is done, return I to my grave
       the tocsin now doth ring its ghastly knell
       prepare thee for thy end: it's time for hell!

*The statue releases its grip. The Don lets out a scream of agony as the ground swallows him up and he is dragged down to the pits of hell. A chorus of demons greets his downfall.*
Demons   O welcome, Don Giovanni, here's our hand
       for now thou art in *Nether Nether Land!*
       down here there is no love nor earthly treasures
       so say farewell to all thy lustful pleasures
       thy life on Earth did show no real ambition
       'twas spent instead in lewdness and coition!
       thy punishment shall be ten years' contrition
       by which time thou art due for thy remission!

          CURTAIN

# L'Elisir d'Amore

Opera in two acts by Gaetano Donizetti. First produced Milan 1832

Nemorino, a young peasant — tenor

Adina, a wealthy farm-owner — soprano

Belcore, an army sergeant — baritone

Dulcamara, a quack doctor — bass

Scene: a village in Italy             Time: 19th century

*Act 1, Scene 1. Adina's farm.*
Nem:  Sweet Adina's such a cutie
      reading books, she's really cool
      blessed with brains as well as beauty
      next to her I look a fool
      How can I ever win her love
      all I can do is sigh
      oh, who will help me, heav'ns above
      I'm such a nerd, I'll cry!
Adina *[reading from book]*
      "Tristan won Isolde's hand
      her beauty was her glory
      fairest maid in all the land."
      Oh, what a silly story!
      "While the moon and stars above
      did witness their emotion
      they did drink 'elixir of love'
      a really potent potion
      In an instant from Isolde
      did her icy coldness fade
      she did fall in love with Tristan
      thus two hearts in one were made!"

      Such an absurd silly notion
      only is in books retold
  *[aside]* but if I can find this potion
      it might turn my life turn to gold!

*A drum roll announces the arrival of the swaggering Sargeant Belcore and his soldiers. Approaching Adina he gallantly presents her with a posy of flowers.*

| | |
|---|---|
| Belcore | Fair lady, I'm not here to bide |
| | my name's Sergeant Belcore |
| | my fame has travelled far and wide |
| | from Bergamo to Torre |
| | I've been a soldier all my life |
| | so do accept this posy |
| | I'd like to have you for my wife |
| [aside] | my future's looking rosy! |
| | |
| Adina [aside] | Audacious as this sergeant is |
| | I must admit he's handsome |
| | ungracious as his manner is |
| | his offer's worth a ransom! |
| [to Belcore] | I have no wish to marry you |
| | you're far below my station |
| [aside] | I think he's met his Waterloo |
| | that's changed the situation!) |

*[Belcore and villagers leave. Nemorino protests his love but Adina is not interested]*

| | |
|---|---|
| Adina | O stop your sighing if you will |
| | your view of life is dim |
| | I hear your uncle's gravely ill |
| | why don't you visit him? |
| | Your lovesick act is boring me |
| | I don't need such devotions |
| | why don't you go and find the key |
| | to unlock magic potions? |

*Scene 2. The village square*
*Dr Dulcamara arrives in his gilded carriage. He tells Nemorino and the villagers of his miraculous cures which he sells for only one scudo.*

| | |
|---|---|
| Nem | Oh doctor, can you tell me well |
| [aside] | (I'm feeling so much bolder) |
| | do you the magic potion sell |
| | that Tristan gave Isolde? |

Dulcamara    My friend, by chance I've got a few
             I make them ev'ry morning
             it's quite a potent little brew
             that's why I give you warning!
*[hands him a bottle of cheap Bordeaux]*
Nem          I'm much obliged for your advice
             how can I ever thank you!
             Before I buy it what's the price
             for now I have to pay you

Dulcamara    One *scudo* is the current price
             none further do I ask
     *[aside]*  I could from him much more entice
             I've got an unsold cask!
  *[to Nemorino]* Remember shake the bottle well
             before you take a sip
             then wait a day for it to gel
     *[aside]*  by then away I'll slip!
*Dulcamara enters the inn. Nemorino shakes the bottle and drinks a draught, then another. This makes him tipsy and he sits down on a nearby bench.*
Nem *[singing*   La-la-la-la-lera, la-la-la-la-la
    *exuberantly]*   la-la-la-la-lera, la-la-la-la etc.

Adina *[piqued]*  Oh what's the reason for his glee
             his manner so elated?
             he doesn't even look at me
             is his love now abated?

Belcore      My dear Adina, have you thought
             about our wedding plans
             your wedding ring's as good as bought
             I'll just set up the banns

Adina        So be it! come, let us be wed
             within this coming week, sir
             Then we'll enjoy the nuptial bed *[glancing at Nemorino]*
             I've no time for the meek, sir!

*Belcore, overjoyed at Adina's acceptance, sends for the notary. A note from the captain arrives ordering him and his men to leave the village the next morning. At Belcore's insistence Adina agrees to marry him immediately. Nemorino pleads with her to wait one more day but she refuses to listen.*

*Act 2 Scene 1*
*A room inside Adina's farmhouse.*

Guests   Hail Adina, queen of beauty,
      of a kindness sweet and rare
      to her husband does she duty
      let us toast the happy pair!

Belcore   I've achieved my life's ambition
      the two pleasures I love strong
      I've accomplishéd my mission
      Wine and women – then a song!

*The notary appears. Nemorino, seeing Dr Dulcamara, explains his desperate situation.*

Nem    O good doctor, you must hurry
      I'm in such an awful plight
      My Adina's set to marry
      someone else this very night!
      I must have another bottle
      of your elixir of love
      if I don't I'll surely tottle
  *[aside]* it's goodbye, my little dove!

Dulcamara Here's a bottle for your pleasure
      just one *scudo* is the cost
      you can buy it at your leisure
  *[aside]* when he's paid me I'll get lost!

*Dulcamara leaves. Adina, piqued at Nemorino's absence, has delayed signing the wedding contract. Belcore finds Nemorino despondent outside the farmhouse.*

Nem    I've got no money for the doc
*[despondently]* I haven't got a sou
      I've nothing I can put in hock
      Oh what am I to do?

Belcore *[aside]* It seems my rival's in a tizz
      behaving strange and funny
      I wonder what his problem is
      perhaps he needs some money!
 *[to Nem]* Cheer up, my friend, don't make a hash
      of life, so don't feel blue
      if what you need's a spot of cash
      the Army's here for you! *[producing paper]*

                        Just write your name or you can sign
                        an 'X', will also do *[Nemorino signs]*
                        you're now enlisted in the line
                        these *scudi* are for you!
    *[Nemorino takes the money]*

Nem *[jubilant]*    Hurrah! hurrah! I've got the cash
                        I need no longer pine
                        to Dulcamara now I'll dash
                        the elixir is mine!
    *[he rushes off to find Dr Dulcamara]*

Belcore             With one fell swoop I've won my case
    *[laughing]*    my rival have I netted
                        he is no longer in the race
                        I've aided and abetted!

*Scene 2. A courtyard. News arrives that Nemorino's rich uncle has died, leaving him a fortune. The village girls, now eager to court him, gather in the courtyard.*

Chorus              What excitement! what a story!
                        Here's the news just in today
                        Nemorino's set for glory
                        his rich uncle's passed away!
                        In his will he left a million:
                        houses, stables, silver plate
                        now his nephew's worth a zillion
                        how I'd love to be his mate!
                        What a catch for village maidens
                        watch them push each one aside!
                        speaking words so honey-laden
                        how they'll rush to be his bride!

*Nemorino enters and is quickly surrounded by the village beauties, which he puts down to the effects of the elixir.*

Nem                 This elixir has kindled hope
                        how quickly these girls found me
                        I need no longer sigh and mope
                        look how they're flirting round me!

*Adina and Dulcamara are astonished to see Nemorino courted by the village girls.*

| | |
|---|---|
| Adina | This sight I see before my eyes |
| | I simply don't believe |
| | the girls are buzzing round like flies |
| | oh how it makes me peeved! |
| | Instead of showing signs of woe |
| | and utterly dejected |
| | he lets me know that I can go |
| | now I'm the one rejected! |
| | |
| Dulcamara | I never knew my magic brew |
| | would prove so efficacious |
| | I have a plan for ev'ry man |
| | that some would call audacious |
| | This simple peasant has the gift |
| | of helping me make money |
| | If I can fifty bottles shift |
| | My future's looking sunny! |
| | |
| Adina | My heart is in a dizzy whirl |
| | I think I've been too clever |
| | He's turned the head of ev'ry girl |
| | I've lost him now forever! |
| | |
| Dulcamara *[aside]* | My reading of the stars above |
| | (as proven by her visit) |
| | with Nemorino she's in love |
| | but too proud to admit it! |
| | |
| Adina *[aside]* | I know a plan to get my man |
| | and make it quite exciting |
| | one tender look, he's on the hook |
| | the rest is just enticing! |

*She approaches Nemorino.*

    Your army contract I have bought
    you're free to leave without it
    A painful lesson I've been taught
    let's say no more about it
    Instead of going off to war
    stay here with those who love you
    I cannot tell you anymore
    except to say I love you!

*Adina tells Belcore that she loves Nemorino and that the wedding is off.*

| | |
|---|---|
| Belcore | It's all the same to me, my sweet |
| | a soldier's life is steady |
| | another girl, another treat |
| | Belcore's always ready! |
| | Brunette today, a blonde the next |
| | a soldier's life is steady |
| | we never know what to expect |
| | Belcore's always ready! |
| | |
| Dulcamara | Farewell, my friends, we'll meet again |
| | but don't forget my potion |
| | it cures the most distressful pain |
| | and acts as body lotion |
| | Who wants a bottle over there? |
| | to you, sir, here are three, |
| | for Dulcamara's cures are rare |
| | and only sold by me! |

*The assembled villagers clamour to buy up his stock. As his carriage drives away they throw their hats into the air and loudly cheer. Adina and Nemorino embrace.*

*CURTAIN*

# Faust

Opera in 5 acts by Charles Gounod.
First produced Paris 1859

| | |
|---|---|
| Faust, an aged philosopher | tenor |
| Mef, the very devil | bass |
| Marguerite (acts 1-3) | light soprano |
| (acts 4-5, or 9 months later) | heavy soprano |
| Valentine, her brother | baritone |
| Siebel, a youth | mezzo |

Students, soldiers, revellers, angels, demons etc

Scene: Germany                    Time: 16$^{th}$ century

*Act 1. Faust's den.*
The aged philosopher Faust is deep in a brown study$_{(1)}$. Life, he says wearily to himself, is *kaputt*, what with the ever-increasing cost of *Bratwurst* and *Bier:* better to end it all. He is about to take an overdose of aspirins when a crowd of revellers passes by. In a deep depression he picks up his cellphone and calls on the Powers of Evil for help. Before you can say *Götterdämmerung* his call is answered: a recorded message asks him to press 1 for Heaven and 2 for Hell. He presses 2 and immediately a tall and curious figure, sporting curly mustachios and an even curlier tail, appears out of a trapdoor and a puff of smoke.

"Who the devil are you?" asks the astonished philosopher. "Right first time, cobber!" replies the insolent rogue in a thick 'down under' accent –clear proof of where he's come from. He then introduces himself as Mef, short for Mefylated Spirit: he was, he explains, an ordinary spirit until he drank mefylated. "What wouldst thou?" he asks the goggled-eyed philosopher, "what can I offer thee? Gold? Girls? A Lamborghini LP560? Speak and it shall be thine!"

Faust replies that all he wants is his youth back. "Done!" cries the visitor, and taking a lease agreement out of his pocket says "just sign here, *si'l vous plait*; terms and conditions apply". He then explains what his terms are. " Pon my soul!" exclaims Faust. "Exactly!" rejoins the devil with a toothless grin. As Faust is still hesitant Mef conjures up a vision of a busty blonde named Marguerite and shows it to the doubting philosopher. Captivated by her 39-26-38 charms, Faust signs eagerly on the dotted line. The pact with the devil is sealed!

(1). producers can use other colours if brown is not available

*Act 2. A village fair.*
The curtain rises on a merry scene showing crowds of villagers eating, drinking and dancing to the strains of *The Howling Groans,* a local pop group. Students and other militants enjoy a noisy noggin outside the *Drei Löwen* while groups of soldiers chat up the local lassies. Among them is Valentine, Marguerite's brother and already much the worse for drink. After downing another stein he gets unsteadily to his feet and holding a medallion in one hand and a *Fräulein* in the other sings *Even bravest heart may swell* but owing to his advanced state of intoxication he only gets as far as the first line.

Next on the scene is Siebel, a youth in love with Marguerite. Like his counterpart in *The Marriage of Figaro,* Siebel can't make up his mind whether to be a boy or a girl: not even the producer is sure. That's why mezzos like to sing the role: they can show off their slim figures in breeches. Siebel promises Valentine he will protect his sister while he's away and the two down another stein in pledge.

Faust and Mef now arrive. Faust goes off for a quick leak and Mef joins the noisy students outside the tavern. Among them is Wagner – he would then have been about 20 –who has a reputation as a political rabble-rouser. Getting up, Wagner bleats out in German the *Song of the Rat*, but after a few bahs is interrupted by Mef. Flinging handfuls of deutschmarks at the delighted mob, he sings the *Calf of Gold,* a cynical song about the Gnomes of Zürich. He then causes wine to flow 'miraculously' from the inn-sign (having secretly connected it earlier to a wine barrel) thereby making himself more suspect with the villagers.

Valentine, by now completely plastered, challenges Mef to a duel but his sword mysteriously breaks in half. The soldiers, recognizing the evil stranger as Satan, hold up their swords so as to form a cross with the handles and Mef cowers away. The village dance begins. Marguerite enters and Faust gallantly offers her his arm, which she declines.

*Act 3. Marguerite's garden.*
Evening of the same day. Siebel enters Marguerite's garden and picks her some marguerites, but as prophesized by Mef, they wither. He then goes to a font and, following the stage directions, dips the flowers in Holy Water but the Props Manager forgot to fill the thing up and the flowers remain withered. In a filthy temper Siebel flings them at Marguerite's door and stumps off to the *Drei Löwen* to drown his sorrows.

Next to appear is Faust. Gazing at Marguerite's humble abode, he sings "All hail, thou dwelling" and in answer to his song, the heavens open up and his top C is drowned in the ensuing hailstorm. Mef enters and with a knowing wink at the audience places a casket of fabulous jewels at Marguerite's door next to Siebel's withered stalk.. The two then retire to await results.

And they're not long in coming. At a sign from the stage manager Marguerite makes her long-awaited appearance. She is shown seated at a spinning-wheel – a Singer, of course – and as she turns the wheel recalls her meeting with the handsome stranger. Who can he be, she muses to herself? is he rich or poor? tenor or bass? Having finished spinning her yarn, she steps outside and picks up Siebel's withered stalk. Then her eyes light upon the casket and in a frenzy of excitement she opens it. *"Mon Dieu!"* she exclaims when she sees the sparklers inside, *"que des bijoux!"* Quickly adorning herself with them she sings the famous Jewel Song, admiring herself in a mirror thoughtfully provided by Mef.

It's now time, as the devil cynically remarks, to get the sex-interest flowing again. Faust approaches the bejewelled maiden and chats her up while Mef obligingly casts a magic spell over the couple, making them oblivious to the world. Marguerite, flattered by Faust's attentions, tells him about herself and Faust, always the gentleman, listens politely. He then escorts her back to the cottage, bidding her a courteous goodnight before leaving.

Marguerite enters the cottage and opening her bedroom window (ground floor, first room on the right) sings of her rapture at her newly found love. Our hero, momentarily forgetting to be the gentleman, rushes to the window and clasps the willing maiden in his arms. With a cry of delight she returns his embrace and is thrilled to find a fellow feeling in her bosom. Unfortunately, in the heat of the moment she forgets to put on her nightcap and we have to wait until the next act to find out what happened at the window.

*Act 4. Scene 1. 'The Church Scene'.*
Nine months later. You don't have to know much about opera to work out what happened at the end of act 3. Although the libretto carefully avoids any mention of Marguerite's condition any five-year old in the audience can tell you the facts: Marguerite is in the family way.

When the curtain rises we see the interior of a church. Marguerite has gone there to pray but is met only by Mef's mocking laughter. Overcome by grief, she falls into a faint. The chorus sings *Ah! Men!* and the curtain falls hurriedly.


*Scene 2. The street outside Marguerite's cottage*
A troop of victorious soldiers, among them Valentine, is returning home from the whores. As they march proudly along the street they sing a rousing chorus to the tune of *Gloire immortelle*, which every schoolboy in France knows, albeit to different words. They stop off at the *Drei Löwen* for a few rounds before returning to the bosoms of their families and those of their girlfriends.

Faust and Mef emerge from the shadows and the latter, strumming a guitar, sings a mocking serenade outside Marguerite's window – the same one that started all the trouble. The window opens, but instead of sister Marguerite brother Valentine appears, and none too pleased either at being woken up. Having learnt the truth about his sister and angered by Mef's insulting words he draws his sword and challenges Faust to a duel, but at a crucial moment he slips on a banana skin skilfully thrown by Mef and is mortally wounded. Marguerite rushes out and bending over her dying brother is just in time to receive a well-aimed spit in the eye before he expires.

*Act 5. Scene 1. The Harz Mountains.*  Usually omitted; we shall do likewise.

*Scene 2. A prison cell*
Marguerite is in clink and condemned to death for having drowned her baby. Faust enters and pleads with her to escape with him but her mind has gone. Mef, who's getting impatient, pokes his head round the door. "Cut the cackle and get yer skates on!" he tells them bluntly, "otherwise we'll be here all bleedin' night!"

At the sight of Mef Marguerite recoils in terror. Faust tries to drag her away but moving 100kg of solid flesh is no easy matter and he gives up. A noisy trio develops during which a baby suddenly begins to bawl its head off. "I thought you drowned the little b******!" Faust yells at Marguerite across the stage. "I did!" she screams back. It's discovered later that the baby belongs to the theatre's char who had left it in the wings and forgotten about it.

Marguerite falls lifeless to the floor.  Mef, believing he has won another soul, rubs his hands with glee (a kind of devilish soap) and pointing to her lifeless body shouts triumphantly *"Damned!"*  *"Shaved!"* shouts back the lisping chorus.  Then, not unlike Hoffnung's celebrated bricklayer story, Marguerite goes slowly up to heaven as the final curtain comes slowly down.

So ends this grandest of French Grand Operas.  It's not clear what happened to Faust, but rumour has it that having acquired a taste for *hell* (light German beer) that's where he went, dragged down by Mef.

# *Fidelio*

Opera in 2 acts and 4 overtures by Beethoven.
First produced Vienna 1805.

| | |
|---|---|
| Florestan, a Spanish nobleman | tenor |
| Leonore, his wife ('Fidelio') | soprano |
| Don Fernando, minister for Human Rights | bass |
| Don Pizzarro, prison governor | baritone |
| Rocco, chief gaoler | bass |
| Marzelline, his daughter | soprano |
| Jacquino, Rocco's assistant | tenor |

Scene: A fortress near Seville    Time: 18$^{th}$ century

*Don Pizzarro has imprisoned Florestan in an underground cell. Leonore, disguised as a man, has got herself a job as assistant gaoler in order to rescue her husband.*

*Act 1. Courtyard of the prison.*
The opera begins with an overture. Which one, you may ask? *Ach,* no one knows! Beethoven composed four and the secret died with him. Just to add to the confusion, no 2 is really no 1 and no 3 is really no 2.

The curtain rises to reveal Jacquino busy chatting up Marzelline, Rocco's daughter. Jacquino, it seems, is in love with her but –and here's the rub – she's not in love with him. Nope, Marzelline is Kopf ober Felse in love with Fidelio, a young man who has come to work as assistant gaoler to her father. What Marzelline doesn't know is that Fidelio is really a woman in disguise, which doesn't say much for her I.Q.

Rocco enters. Like his daughter, the old gaoler also doesn't know that Fidelio is a woman in disguise and in fact is almost ready to accept him as a future son-in-law. Needless to say, neither Jacquino nor Fidelio are too happy about this. Fidelio now enters and as part of this Eternal Triangle Beethoven has composed an Eternal Quartet, in which each character expresses his/her feelings on the subject.

Don Pizzarro appears. He posts a trumpeter to alert him of the Minister's approach and orders his soldiers guarding the road from Seville that if a certain meddling barber is spotted he is to be shot on sight. The governor now opens his despatch box. *Gott in Himmel!* he exclaims: Don Fernando, the Minister for Human Rights, is coming today to inspect his prison. If Florestan is found, *Alles ist kaputt!* Florestan must die.

The governor tries to bribe Rocco to do the deed, but when the gaoler refuses Don Pizzaro resolves to do the hatchet job himself. By a strange coincidence rare in opera their conversation is overheard by Leonore, who believing that the unknown prisoner is her husband, vows to rescue him or die in the attempt. She expresses her feelings in the aria *Komm Hoffnung* which, it is said, Beethoven wrote in memory of the famous British cartoonist, musician and wit.

It's now time for the prisoners' coffee break. As they stream out of their dark cells into the bright sunlight they sing the celebrated Prisoners' Chorus, in which the younger ones sing *ff*, punctuated by an occasional *pp* from the older ones. Leonore scans their faces in the hope of finding Florestan among them, but in vain. She learns, however, from Rocco that she is to help him dig a grave for an unknown prisoner. When Don Pizzaro returns he harshly orders the prisoners back to their cells, *doppel schnell.*

*Act 2. Scene 1: An underground cell.*
After our eyes have become accustomed to the darkness we can make out the huddled figure of Florestan fastened by a chain to the wall. This is to make sure he's ready for his big aria, the previous tenor having arrived halfway through the second act. Although Florestan has been imprisoned for two years he's only just discovered how dark it is, hence his opening words *Gott! welch' Dunkel hier!*

Rocco and Fidelio now descend the stairs and begin to dig a grave. As they enter Florestan stirs and Fidelio, catching sight of him for the first time, has difficulty in recognizing this emaciated, feeble-looking man as her husband. She offers him some wine and a morsel of bread, which he gratefully accepts.

Don Pizzarro enters. Dismissing Rocco and Fidelio from the scene the evil governor reveals to the prisoner who he is and raises his dagger, but before you can say *Bundeskraftposthalteseellen-zeichenunterhalt-swärterlehrling* Fidelio,who has returned to the dungeon unseen, throws herself in front of the prisoner and, drawing a pistol, cries *Töt 'erst sein Weib!* Just then a trumpet call rings out: the Minister has arrived! Don Pizzarro hurries out to meet him while husband and wife, reunited at long last, fall rapturously into each other's arms.

*Scene 2. The prison square.*
Amid scenes of much rejoicing the prisoners are freed. The Minister recognises Florestan as his long-lost friend whom he had feared dead. The wicked Don Pizzarro is led away under guard and the opera closes with the chorus singing a joyous hymn in praise of Leonore's bravery and her devotion to the cause of Womens' Lib.

# Die Fledermaus

Operetta in 3 acts by Johann Strauss.  First produced Vienna 1874.

| | |
|---|---|
| Gabriel von Eisenstein, a rich gent | tenor |
| Rosalinde, his wife | soprano |
| Adèle, her maid | soprano |
| Alfred, a singer | tenor |
| Frank, prison governor | baritone |
| Orlofsky, a rich Russian prince | mezzo |
| Dr Falke, Eisenstein's friend | baritone |
| Dr Blind, Eisenstein's attorney | tenor |
| Frosch, a jailer | speaking part |
| Scene: Vienna | Time: ca 1870 |

*Act 1. Eisenstein's house. Alfred's voice offstage.*
Alfred  O hear my plaintive song of love,
O nothing let it hinder
I sing it to my turtle-dove,
my darling Rosalinde
when we were lovers without guile,
both you and I were happy
just leave your hubby for a while,
he's so inept and crappy!

*[enter Adèle reading a letter]*
Adèle  Dear sister Ida writes to say:
"Now listen to my story
tonight if you can get away
you'll find both fame and glory
a splendid party's been announced
at Prince Orlofsky's palace
just wear a gown with lots of flounce,
the entertainment's lavish!

*[enter Rosalinde hurriedly]*
Rosa  That tenor voice not far away
is Alfred's, pure and simple
I recognise his thrilling A,
it fairly makes me tingle
his luscious tones just turn my head,
my passion they do kindle
my thoughts of faith are now misled,
o that I were still single!

Adèle *[tearfully]*
O madam, please your maid forgive,
my aunt's so ill and weary
she may not have much time to live,
her life's become so dreary
I'd like to visit her tonight,
it can't wait for the morrow
for as her niece I feel it's right,
may I this evening borrow?

Rosa *[crossly]*  I really cannot be delayed,
I can make no decision
my husband's supper must be laid,
before he goes to prison
for five days will he tarry there,
without my supervision *[aside]*

                    it's truly more than I can bear,
                    I'm in a tight position!
*[enter Eisenstein in a bad mood with Dr Blind]*
Eisen               You are an utter numbskull, man,
                    you sorely make me wonder
                    it's thanks to you I'm in this jam,
                    a mighty stupid blunder
                    instead of five days I've got eight,
                    a figure of derision
                    I'll have to tell my wife I'm late,
                    before I go to prison
*[enter Dr Falke]*
Falke*[aside]*      That fancy dress ball was the key,
                    three years I've spent in waiting
                    revenge has come at last to me,
                    gone are my days of hating
                    This Eisenstein on me did play
                    a dirty trick, (the rat!)
                    He let me by the roadside lay,
                    still costumed as a bat!
*[to Eisenstein]*   Some splendid news to make you whirl:
                    we're going to a party
                    there's lots of gorgeous dancing girls,
                    so dress up and be smarty
                    When Prince Orlofsky gives a ball
                    you know you're in the pink
                    tomorrow morning leave it all
                    and make your way to 'clink!' *[exit]*
*[enter Rosalinde]*
Rosa                Oh Gabriel, what's going on?
                    these garments have I brought you
                    I thought you'd like to try them on,
                    for prison wear they'll suit you

Eisen *[elated]*    A change of plan there's been, no less
                    a change in garments too
                    to change into my evening dress
                    is what I plan to do *[goes off to change]*

*[Rosalinde gives Adèle the evening off; Eisenstein leaves for the party. Alfred appears and seeing the table laid for supper sits down and helps himself]*
Alfred appears      Your hubby's off to prison gone
                    so do relax, my sweet

                his dressing gown shall I put on
                while you the coffee heat
                for breakfast I would like beef roast
                some caviar and cream
                one slice at most of buttered toast
                then cuddle up and dream!

Rosa         Oh Alfred, you must really fly
                this joke's gone far enough
                a married woman now am I
                or I'll with you get tough!

*[A noise is heard outside;Governor Frank enters; seeing Alfred seated at the table he assumes he is Eisenstein and prepares to to escort him to jail]*
Frank        Dear lady, I regret to say
                within your very house
                that I have come to take away
                your honest, loving spouse
                for eight whole days he'll be my guest
                at Vienna's finest jail
                I will ensure he gets the best
                of that I will not fail!
   *[to Alfred]*   It's time to say farewell to friends
                my men do outside wait
                we have a new Mercedes-Benz
                to take you there in state
                The journey should not cause you pain
                it's only seven miles
                and when you come back home again
                your wife will be all smiles!

Alfred       Before I leave you, darling wife
                there's something I insist
                no scenes to show of married strife
                but just a farewell kiss
*[he kisses Rosalinde passionately]*
    *[aside]*    I think I'll grab another one
                I've never felt so well
  *[he kisses her again]*

so now I sing my little song
                'Mein Liebchen, trinke schnell!'

*Act 2. Prince Orlofsky's party.*

| | |
|---|---|
| Falke | I trust Your Highness will enjoy<br>my well planned little game<br>I've made good use of ev'ry ploy<br>to help achieve my aim |
| *[aside]* | but where the deuce is Eisenstein<br>essential to my plan?<br>it's now a quarter after nine<br>and still can't see the man! |

*[enter Eisenstein disguised as the Marquis de Renard]*

| | |
|---|---|
| Falke | Your Highness, may I now present<br>the Marquis de Renard<br>a Frenchman who's on pleasure bent<br>and loves his caviar |
| Prince | Dear Marquis, you are welcome, sir<br>the party's not begun *[aside]*<br>but when it does, we may be sure<br>we're in for lots of fun! *[to Falke]*<br>my motto that I ne'er forget<br>and e'er regard as true<br>is "However sticky life can get<br>*chacun à son goo!*" |
| Eisen<br>  *[to Falke]* | I'm sure that person is Adèle<br>among these honoured guests<br>but why she's dressed up as a swell<br>in Rosalinde's dress? |
| Falke | My dear Marquis, don't be absurd<br>you've had too much to drink<br>your servant girl's no social bird<br>she's at her kitchen sink<br>I beg you not to make a scene<br>it would be most improper<br>so first explain just what you mean<br>before you drop a whopper! |

*[Adele joins them]*

| | |
|---|---|
| Adèle | A shocking gaffe, my friend, you've made<br>and may I add ill graced<br>to say that I'm your serving maid<br>displays such vulgar taste |

My name is Olga, yes, that's me
and I can sing and dance
an actress I was born to be
by destiny, not chance!

*[Rosalinde, heavily masked and disguised as a Hungarian countess, is announced]*

Eisen      O what a beauty to behold
a countess too, they say
I'm sure she's worth her weight in gold
I'll chat her right away *[to Rosalinde]*
Dear countess, here's a little watch
Just listen to its tick *[aside]*
another conquest soon I'll notch
my charm will do the trick!

Rosa      I'd love to have a watch like that
that measures heartbeats so *[aside]*
this proves my husband's such a rat
how can he stoop so low?
With that watch mine his fate is bought
his flirting I will nail
with evidence like that in court
he'll get six months in jail!

*[Rosalinde succeeds in keeping the watch much to Eisenstein's annoyance]*

Adèle      O countess, in your Magyar lace
and please excuse my asking
we cannot see your lovely face
please show us by unmasking
and then do charm us with a song
about your native land
 where Magyars feel that they belong
and chivalry is grand!

Rosa      My mask, my dear, I can't remove
to do so is improper
but sing a song is in the groove
and that I'll gladly offer *[sings Csardas]*

Prince      And now, dear friends, let's not be vain,
We'll toast the king of wines
just charge your glasses with champagne
and drink to all that's fine

| | |
|---|---|
| Falke | Another toast I'd like to do<br>'Fond brotherhood' to reign<br>let all here present 'Du-i-du'<br>before we drink again! |
| Chorus | O Brüderlein, o Schwesterlein<br>forever will remain<br>we must admit the King of Wine<br>will always be champagne! |

*[a clock strikes six]*

| | | |
|---|---|---|
| Eisen | | The clock has struck, it's time I went |
| | *[aside]* | how can I leave this charmer? |
| Rosa | *[aside]* | O husband dear, your fate is spent<br>for now begins the drama! |

Act 3. The prison.
*[Frosch, blind drunk, hears Alfred's voice and turns on him angrily]*

| | |
|---|---|
| Frosch | That prisoner in number twelve<br>without his tie and jacket<br>into his umpteen songs does delve<br>and makes a fearful racket<br>Hey, you in there, in dressing gown<br>can't you behave all proper?<br>don't sing so much and keep it down<br>this hain't the Royal Opera! |

*[Governor Frank, also half drunk, enters and looks about him]*

| | |
|---|---|
| Frank | So here I am, after my gap<br>well fortified by wine<br>I think I'll have a little nap<br>and then see Eisenstein *[falls asleep]* |

*[The doorbell rings. Frosch admits Adèle and Ida]*

| | |
|---|---|
| Ida | We're looking for a noble gent<br>a Chevalier Chagrin<br>to this address we have been sent<br>so can you find this man? |

Frosch *[to Frank]*
                Beg pardon, sir, this hain't a joke
                two ladies wait within
                they're lookin' for a foreign bloke
                who calls 'imself Sha-grin

| Frank | I wonder who they want to meet |
| | so early in the day *[sees Adèle and Ida]* |
| | Good morning, ladies, take a seat |
| *[aside]* | I hope they'll go away! |

| Ida | We've come to ask you, sir, don't rage |
| | to help my sis Adèle |
| | she longs to act upon the stage |
| | and knows she'll do quite well |

*[Doorbell rings again. Enter Eisenstein still dressed as Marquis de Renard]*
| Frank | My dear Marquis! Is this a prank? |
| | you're looking well and hearty |
| | I should explain my name is Frank |
| | 'Chagrin' was for the party |

| Eisen | My sentence I have come to serve |
| | that's why I'm here on time |
| | from duty I've no wish to swerve |
| | my name is Eisenstein! |

| Frank | My dear Marquis, you are a card! |
| | the best joke of the year |
| | your sense of humour learn to guard |
| | for Eisenstein's right here! *[points to cell no.12]* |

*[Doorbell rings again. Rosalinde, heavily veiled, enters to get Alfred out before her husband arrives. Eisenstein, curious to know who was arrested in his place, quickly disguises himself as Dr Blind and proceeds to cross examine Rosalinde and Alfred].*
| Eisen *[gruffly]* | Give me the basic facts, my friend, |
| | that's all I need from you |
| | and please remember not to bend |
| | the truth, or you'll be through |

| Alfred | "It all began, there was no plan |
| | when we at supper met |
| | I sat down in this dressing gown |
| | we had a tête-à-tête |
| | Out of the blue, next thing I knew |
| | my person was mistaken |
| | and tho into a rage I flew |
| | I was to prison taken! |

| | |
|---|---|
| Rosa | My husband's heading for a fall |
| | he thinks he's king of chancers |
| | last night at Prince Orlofsky's ball |
| | I saw him flirt with dancers! |

Eisen        I think that I can now unwind
　　　　　　your case is clearly 'Nein'
　　　　　　I'll show you I'm no longer Blind
　　*[takes off coat, wig etc]*
　　　　　　I'm Gabriel Eisenstein!

Rosa　　　　Another of his dirty tricks
　　　　　　but this one too I'll scotch
　　*[dangling watch and putting on Hungarian accent]*
　　　　　　"O marquis, listen to zeese ticks
　　　　　　it's zuch a charming vatch!"

Eisen *[aside]* A fool I've been, I've met my match
　　　　　　last night has changed my life
　　　　　　I thought that I had made a catch
　　　　　　instead it was my wife!

　　*[enter Dr Falke, the Prince, chorus etc]*
Falke　　　　My brilliant plan has worked out well
　　　　　　revenge, so sweet, is mine
　　　　　　if I can be that 'bat from hell'
　　　　　　it's thanks to Eisenstein!

Prince　　　Dear friends at last this little game
　　　　　　has come to its sweet end
　　　　　　another glass of French champagne
　　　　　　before we homeward wend!

　　　　　　　　*CURTAIN*

# Der Freischütz

Opera in 3 acts by Carl Maria von Weber.
First produced Berlin 1821.

| | |
|---|---:|
| Max, a ranger, in love with Agathe | tenor |
| Caspar, a forester | bass |
| Cuno, head ranger | bass |
| Agathe, his daughter | soprano |
| Scene: Bohemia | Time: 17$^{th}$ century |

*Act 1. A shooting range. Villagers congratulate Kilian, a peasant, on beating Max, a ranger.*

Villagers  Young Kilian's done the trick, no doubt about it
      his bullet hit the mark, went right on target!

Max (gloomily) My chances at the shooting range I've fumbled
      the shooting skills I had have all but tumbled
      the good luck I enjoyed has fully crumbled
      all hope of winning Agathe I've bumbled
      on top of that, and this I find unpleasant
      that ranger Max's been beaten by a peasant!

Cuno    If you don't win the shooting match tomorrow
      poor Agathe will be really full of sorrow!

Casper *[to Max]*
      Cheer up, young man, I'll help you win the contest
      do what I say and you shall have your conquest
      now take this gun, it's absolutely legal
      take careful aim and shoot yon flying eagle!

*[Max shoots; the eagle falls from a great height dead at his feet. Max is amazed]*
      You see, my friend, what magic bullets do
      with just one shot they'll make your dreams come true
      at midnight come alone to the Wolf's Glen
      we'll make the magic bullets in my den!

*[Max, excited at the prospect of winning the contest and Agatha's hand, readily agrees]*
Casper *[aside]* My rival I've entwined into the net
      revenge at last is mine, the die is set
      of evil machinations I'm the Mago
      I'm better at intrigue than was Iago!

*Act 2 Scene 1. Cuno's house. Agathe is troubled by gloomy forebodings. Max enters.*

Max    I've just come by to tell you not to fear
      to Wolf's Glen I am off to claim the deer
      I shot the other morning by the stream
      it really was a beauty, not a dream!

Agatha   My dearest Max, I know you're quite undaunted
      go not to the Wolf's Glen, they say it's haunted

>    the vibes I get have set my mind a-reeling
>    while in my heart I've got a funny feelng!

*[Despite Agathe's entreaties Max leaves and makes his way to the Wolf's Glen]*

*Scene 2. Midnight in The Wolf's Glen. Caspar, standing inside a circle of stones, is moulding bullets using a crucible, a casting ladle and a mould. Max enters.*

Caspar  
>    Come in, my friend, just grab a scotch and soda
>    then help me cast this stuff into the loader
>  *[adds ingredients]*
>    first is the lead, then glass from church retaken
>    some quicksilver, from doctors' labs forsaken
>  *[packs into mould]*
>    here's bullet one, ejected from the mould
>    just keep it safe, it's worth its weight in gold!

*[Caspar proceeds to cast seven bullets, six of which go to Max. The seventh goes to Zamiel, an evil spirit to whom Caspar has sold his soul]*

*Act 3. Scene 1. Cuno's house. Agathe, dressed as a bride, relates a strange dream.*

Agathe  
>    I dreamt that I became a dove
>    so white and pure in heaven
>    I flew on trees, below, above
>    I felt 'twas on Cloud Seven
>    Max raised his gun up to the sun
>    the shot rang out like thunder
>    I, in my dream, let out a scream
>    But I escaped, o wonder!

*Scene 2. The shooting contest. Max has used up his bullets during a morning hunt and has only one left. The target is a white dove. As he takes aim Agathe enters. Seeing Max with gun raised and remembering her dream she cries out in alarm.*

Agathe  
>    Oh do not shoot, dear Max, for it is I
>    who am inside that dove high in the sky
>    put down your gun at once, I see it gleam
>    a deadly warning came in last night's dream!

*Max pulls the trigger. Agathe falls but it is Caspar who, hiding in a tree, falls to the ground, fatally wounded. Max's last bullet, which Caspar intended for Agathe, has killed him instead. Max confesses his involvement to Cuno but is pardoned.*

# The Ballad of La Gioconda

Opera in 4 acts by Amilcare Ponchielli. First produced Milan 1876

| | |
|---|---|
| Bárnaba, a spy, in love with | baritone |
| La Gioconda, a ballad singer, in love with | soprano |
| Enzo, a Genoese noble, in love with | tenor |
| Laura, wife of Alvise, not in love with | mezzo |
| Alvise Badoero, Inquisition leader | bass |
| La Cieca, La Gioconda's blind mother | alto |

Scene: Venice     Time: 17$^{th}$ century

*Act 1*

A loathsome spy, corrupt and sly
was Bárnaba of Venice
tho' filled with zest he was a pest
and worked for the Secret Service

His daily job was to spy on the mob
a dirty and dangerous mission
The info he got, whether valid or not
he gave to the dread Inquisition

This spy with a name was in love with a dame
who was known in the town as Gioconda
but when unexpected his love was rejected
he vowed he would make her surrender

The means that he used, which he quickly abused
was to have her blind mother arrested
by reason of which she was branded a witch
a contention Gioconda contested

But Laura, Al's wife, kindly saved Cieca's life
(tho' crippled and blind was she)
and tho' time was pressing gave Laura her blessing
as well as a rosary

Now the spy's hated foe was this fellow Enzo
to whom Bárnaba made a proposal
that Laura would kip from tonight on his ship
thereby sealing the lovers' betrothal

Then to Badoer's palace sped the spy full of malice
and gave Al a report on the lowdown
and with many a lashing and with gnashing teeth flashing
did Alvise concoct a great showdown

But from inside a passage Gioconda did manage
to hear all their devilish dealings
and tho' by Enzo rejected she left undetected
to warn him of Badoer's feelings

*Act 2*

On board his ship doth Enzo wait
for Laura's sweet arrival
but hid on deck is a dame by heck
who's clearly Laura's rival

For Gioconda doth wave a most murderous blade
(an unladylike thing to do)
and has ev'ry intention, despite intervention
to cut up her rival in two

But when she doth see that her mum's rosary
'round Laura's fair neck is adorning
she changes her tack and takes her knife back
and gives Enzo and Laura good warning

*Act 3*

Alvise with scorn a swift vengeance has sworn
on fair Laura, his ill-fated wife
and while at the sink he doth give her to drink
a slow poison, thus ending her life

But Gioconda, unseen, who hath witnessed this scene
swops the drink for a harmless narcotic
and while Laura's asleep in a slumberous deep
old Alvise becomes quite neurotic!

For fully believing that Laura is leaving
this world, round her bier laid he flowers
then inviting friends all to a grandiose ball
they advance to the Dance of the Hours

By this time our Enzo, a fair-minded fellow
begins to behave like a hero
for when it's revealed that fair Laura's been killed
he denounces her husband Badoero

But when Enzo's molested and later arrested
and Bárnaba triumphs with glee
Gioconda agrees that she'll give herself: please
if the spy will let Enzo go free

*Act 4*

The lovers, now that all is well
do watch the ship cast anchor
Gioconda waves a last farewell
all they can do is thank her

Gioconda having said goodbye
doth weepeth as they go
for very soon this dreaded spy
will claim his quid pro quo

Yet long before she'd reach her door
she'd reached a brave decision
between her breasts a clasp-knife rests
prepared to do its mission

With arms outstretch'd the spy expects
to best receive her passion
she with a lunge the blade did plunge
into herself, Tosca fashion!

The spy did swear and tear his hair
too late!  the deed was done
for as tried to grab a hold
he found she'd 'holed' in one!

"I'm thine! I'm thine!" was her last line
no other did she utter
and with a blink he watched her sink
into a nearby gutter


"Thy mother have I murder'd!" shouts
the spy to La Gioconda
but 'twas in vain, for this terrain
she'd left, for one o'er yonder

So ends this hoary and gory story
of lust and things improper
I must confess that such a mess
is only found in Opera!

# Hamlet

Opera in 5 acts by Ambroise Thomas. First produced Paris 1868

Principal characters
Hamlet, prince of Denmark						baritone

Orphelia, daughter of Polonius					soprano

Claudius, king of Denmark						bass

Gertrude, Hamlet's mother						mezzo

Scene: Denmark					Time: 16$^{th}$ century

Act 1.
Scene 1. Elsinore Castle. Hamlet is angered by the marriage of Claudius and Gertrude.

Ham  *[alone]*  This hasty marriage leaves me much disgusted
I fear my uncle's' actions can't be trusted
when father died my uncle seemed unflustered
 but very soon he after mother lusted!

His scheming brain did hatch the plan he'd readied
the queen consented to the step I dreaded
now see the bridal couple, newly wedded *[aside]*
he lost no time in getting Gertrude bedded!

*Orphelia enters, lost in thought. She is distraught by Hamlet's seeming indifference.*

Good morrow, sweet Orphelia, art thou troubled?
thy usual gentle mien doth seem befuddled!

Orph  'Tis naught, my lord, I'm ever pale and swoony
and when I sing my Mad Scene I go loony! *[aside]*
this see-thru top I'm wearing's rather trendy
without me bra he'll find I'm "user-friendly"!

Ham  Thy top's real cool and really most revealing
it's knocked me flat, I feel my senses reeling
Here at thy feet I humbly go down kneeling
let's sing of love, it's such a fellow-feeling!
    *[they sing duet]*

Both  With this duet o let us love forever
deny the light but not the sun its splendour
for thee alone I live, o never doubt it
such love I have for thee, I'm lost  without it!
    *[Exit Orphelia]*

*[Horatio and Marcellus tell Hamlet that his father's ghost appeared to them and that Hamlet is to meet him at midnight]*

Scene 2. The castle battlements. As midnight strikes the ghost appeareth to Hamlet.
Ghost  How fares it, son? I'm here to bid thee welcome
at ten I tried to SMS through Telkom
what I'm about to tell thee keep well girded *[sotto voce]*
'twas Claudius my brother me hath murdered!

			One day, while in my orchard I did slumber
			and dreaming of past pleasures without number
			thy uncle, filled with cruelty so vile
			did pour onto my lips a poison phial
			which, coursing through my veins did end my life
			and took away my kingdom and my wife!

			Avenge, my son, this foul and gruesome killing
			whose very thought doth make it so spine-chilling
			but when thou doth avenge this deed so dirty
			o promise me no harm doth come to Gertie!

Ham		Thy word is my command, o dearest pa
			this villain and his crime shalt not get far
			methinks I have a plan when, put in motion
			will wreak revenge on he who poured the potion!

Act 2.
Scene 1. The castle grounds. Hamlet, meeting Orphelia, departs hastily. Orphelia is sad.
Orph		Alas! I feel that I have been forsaken
			that Hamlet's love for me is overtaken
			I promised him my heart to prove love conquers
			but now it seems he's gone completely bonkers!

Gert		'Tis not the time, Orphelia, for a weepie
			there is no doubt that Hamlet loves thee deeply
			there's still much good in him, he has no badness
			but ev'ry now and then he's touched by madness!
	[exit Orphelia]

The king and queen are alarmed that Hamlet may have discovered evidence of their crime. When he announces that a group of actors will entertain the court they leave reassured.
The actors enter and receive his instructions.
Ham		Good day, kind friends, and welcome to the palace [pours
wine]		a word, I pray, before we drain this chalice
			Tonight you are to re-enact in dumb show
			that splendid play The Murder of Gonzago.
			The play's to be performed before the King [aside]
			we'll see the chain reaction it will bring! [to actors]
			And now, dear friends, pray join me in a toast
			to noble wine, the drink we Danes love most!

> "Dispel, o wine, from my poor heart this sadness
> the time will come when I'm accused of madness!"

*Scene 2. The great hall of the castle. The king, queen and courtiers assemble. Hamlet explains the dumb show on stage: an old king, wearing a crown, enters on the arm of his queen. After he falls asleep a figure enters and with the queen's connivance gives the king a poisoned cup. The courtiers hold their breath.*

Ham   See how the cunning traitor slowly enters
     and pours the deadly poison thro' his dentures!
     the deed is done; watch how he steals the crown
     from off the head and place it on his own!

King *[rising in* Dismiss these wretched actors from this court
   *a frenzy]* destroy the evil factors they have wrought
     whoever planned this reason shall be sought
     a charge of flagrant treason shall be brought!

*Hamlet, feigning madness, points to the king.*
Ham   See now the guilty one himself betrayed
     and how the fatal dose itself was made
     instead of staying calm and e'er realistic
     he shows his guilt by going all ballistic!
     You see him now, his false crown on his head
     upon my soul I wish that he were dead!

*Hamlet approaches the king and tears the crown off his head. The court is thrown into confusion with the king and queen rushing from the hall. Hamlet, hysterical, collapses.*

*Act 3. Scene 1. The queen's chamber with two portraits of Hamlet's father and uncle.*
Ham   I had my chance to kill the fiend but missed it
     what made me stay my hand
       and damn well glitched it?
     To be or not to be, that's not the question
     the answer's sure to give me indigestion!
     But soft! I hear a footstep on the stair
     Methinks I'd better hide, I know not where!
*[he hides behind an arras]*

*The king enters and approaching the pri-Dieu kneels in prayer.*
King   My brother's death hath made me really hated
     before I bumped him off I should have waited

      'twas Gertrude who insisted we get mated
      now I'm accused of having fornicated!

*Hamlet overhears a conversation between the king and Polonius proving that Orphelia's father is also implicated in the murder. When they leave the queen and Orphelia enter.*

Queen *[joyously]*
      Rejoice, dear Hamlet, I welcome now as daughter
      thy bride Orphelia who'll meet thee at the altar
      henceforth thy fate and hers will be united
      all Denmark will rejoice, thy troth be plighted!

Ham *[defiantly]* I shall not wed, tho' you may find it galling
      the chips are down, I go to higher calling
 *[to Orphelia]* the dream that thou didst cherish was in clover
      now get thee to a nunn'ry, thy dream is over!

Orph  *[sadly]* The love that thou didst bear me was my pride
      Oh! how I prayed our love-knot would be tied!
      but now that truth and honour are denied
      my girlish dreams have just curled up and died!

Queen *[to Hamlet]*
      I know not what in heaven's name obsessed thee
      or what satanic thoughts have now possessed thee
      how cruelly, poor Orphelia, didst thou mock her *[aside]*
      it's clear my son is really off his rocker!

*Orphelia departs in tears. After a long silence the Queen addresses Hamlet.*
Queen    Thy father thou hast mortally offended
      'tis only meet this conflict must be mended
      thy mother grieves in silence and in sorrow
      I pray your senses cometh back tomorrow

*Hamlet, pointing to the two portraits on the wall, angrily addresses the queen.*
      This picture is my father, how I wept
      the day that he was murdered as he slept
      the many virtues he possessed are clearly shown:
      nobility and courage and renown
      This other shows a different kind of man:
      deceit, intrigue and murder are his plan!

*The lamp suddenly goes out. The ghost appears and after reminding Hamlet to avenge his death and spare the queen, disappears. The queen is left trembling with fear.*

*Act 4. Orphelia, wearing a long white robe, wanders about the lakeside. In her madness she imagines she has married Hamlet and is now his wife.*

Orph          Now that to Hamlet I am truly wed
                    the joys of married bliss I'll find in bed
                    According to messieurs Barbier and Carré
                    Orphelia sings a song about *Le Villi!*

*She lowers herself into the water and drowns; the current gently carries her away.*

*Act 5. The cemetery of Elsinore. Two comic gravediggers are preparing a fresh grave.*

$1^{st}$              We dig from six to four, ten hours a day
                    we dig down six feet deep, through sand and clay

$2^{nd}$             The coffins come in different shapes and sizes
                    in black, in white, in brown, all kinds of guises

Both          We dig an' dig an' dig right through the day
                    we get just fifteen quid in take-home pay!
                    we want to chuck our job, we're on the brink
                    our only bleedin' pleasure is to drink!
*[they drinketh wine]*

*Hamlet, unaware of Orphelia's death, sees a funeral cortège enter with her body laid out on a bier. The ghost, now visible to all, tells him the time has come to avenge his murder.*

Ghost        O Hamlet, gird thy loins, prepare for action
                    it's time thy sacred oath had satisfaction
                    unsheathe thy blade, and with a deadly thrust
                    despatch the fiend and send him unto dust!

*Hamlet doth obey his father's wish and slays Claudius. The ghost departs and Hamlet is proclaimed king. In an alternative ending Hamlet, mortally wounded, kills Claudius then throws himself upon Orphelia's bier and dies.*

*CURTAIN*

# Les Huguenots

Grand opera in 5 acts by Meyerbeer. First produced Paris 1836

| | |
|---|---|
| Marguerite de Valois, Queen of France | soprano |
| Urbain, her page | mezzo |
| Comte de St Bris, a Catholic leader | bass |
| Valentine, his daughter | soprano |
| Comte de Nevers, engaged to Valentine | baritone |
| Raoul de Nangis, a Huguenot nobleman | tenor |
| Marcel, his servant | bass |

Scene: France                                    Time: 1572

*Historical Note*
Les Huguenots takes place in 16$^{th}$ century France, which is racked by violent religious wars. It also boasts a hero who must be the most dim-witted tenor in opera.


*Act 1. Comte de Nevers' chateau in Touraine.*
The Comte de Nevers is entertaining a group of young Catholic noblemen. One of them, feeling a bit peckish, demands to know when *le diner* will be served, but de Nevers tells him they're waiting for Raoul de Nangis, a Huguenot, to arrive. In the meantime the others tell each other racy stories of their amorous adventures.

The missing guest arrives and food and wine are served. When all are seated de Nevers proposes a toast to *'nos maitresses'* - best translated as something between a master and a mattress. When Raoul is asked for a story about his *amours* he relates how he had rescued an unknown beauty from a group of militant students protesting about increased varsity fees. Although Raoul knows neither her name, rank or station he believes she is from the Gare du Lyon. His aria, *'Plus blanche que la blanche'*, a song in praise of detergents, is considered the forerunner of French Soap Opera.

Raoul's old retainer Marcel enters. Fiercely anti-Catholic, anti-social and antiquated, Marcel strongly disapproves of his master frequenting such 'enemy' circles and sings a defiant Huguenot battle-cry that embarrasses Raoul and succeeds in boring the pants off everyone present, audience included.

A servant enters and tells de Nevers that a veiled lady wishes to speak to him alone in the garden. Filled with curiosity the guests peep through the curtains to catch a glimpse of the mysterious visitor. When it's Raoul's turn he starts back in anger. *Tiens!* for it is none other than the unknown beauty he had rescued earlier. Believing her to be de Nevers' mistress, he feels betrayed. When de Nevers rejoins the guests he tells them that the fair visitor was his fiancée, come to ask to be released from her marriage vows. Being a gentleman he had gallantly agreed to her request.

Just then Urbain, the Queen's page, appears. He bears a message from Her Majesty instructing Raoul to be blindfolded and to accompany some masked men to an unknown destination. He agrees, is blindfolded and led away, to the wonder and admiration of the assembled guests.

*Act 2. The gardens of the chateau of Chenonçeaux.*
Queen Marguerite is surrounded by her ladies in waiting. Raoul, rather like Samson in act 3, is led in, but instead of being blinded, he is merely blindfolded. Moments later his blindfold is removed and the Queen dismisses her ladies, so that she can be alone with him. Unaware that he is in the presence of the Queen – how dumb can a tenor get? – he kneels before her and tells her how beautiful she is. Her Majesty is not displeased with these attentions but for the sake of the opera gets on with the story.

Having exacted a promise that he is to obey her every wish the Queen reveals her plan: in order to end the bitter feud raging between Catholics and Huguenots she has arranged for Raoul to marry Valentine, daughter of the Catholic leader St Bris. After Raoul has consented the Queen orders that Catholic and Huguenot nobles be allowed to enter, among them St Bris, who presents his beautiful daughter.

And it is here that our dumb hero upsets the royal applecart. By one of those rare coincidences in opera his bride-to-be is none other than – guess who? - the unknown beauty de Nevers was chatting up earlier and obviously his mistress! Raoul recoils in anger. Marry her, he tells the Queen? you must be joking! *Quelle perfidie! Jamais!*

The Queen and Valentine cannot believe their ears. As for St Bris and his followers, they are so enraged at this insult to the family honour that they draw their swords. It is only through the Queen's intervention that Raoul is saved from becoming a new dish in *la cuisine française: Huguenot haché à la Touraine.* At the Queen's command Raoul gives up his sword and the act closes with the furious St Bris and de Nevers swearing vengeance as they drag the fainting Valentine away.

*Act 3. The Pré-aux-Clercs meadow in Paris.*
The scene of act 3 is laid, as were countless *belles de nuit,* in the meadow of the Pré-aux-Clercs in Paris. Groups of soldiers, monks, nuns and other lowpaid extras mill about while students and other militant groups stroll around.

A bridal procession enters. Valentine, rejected by Raoul, has married de Nevers, but owing to her poor French her protestations of *Never! Never!* were misunderstood. She enters a nearby chapel and kneels silently in prayer for whatever young brides pray for on their wedding-night.

And it is here that Valentine proves her great love for Raoul. While at prayer she chances to overhear a conversation between two men and to her horror recognises her father and another Catholic follower. They are plotting to ambush Raoul and murder him during a duel to be held at midnight. *Quelle horreur!*

After the two have left Valentine cautiously emerges from behind a pillar. By a strange coincidence who does she bump into but Marcel, who just at that moment is emerging from the *other* side of the pillar. In agitated tones she implores Marcel to warn his master that *oui,* he is in mortal danger and *non,* he must not attend the duel alone.

Marcel rushes off to warn Raoul of the planned treachery and to muster support from fellow Huguenots.

It is midnight: the hour of the duel has arrived. Accompanied by their seconds Raoul and St Bris enter and drawing their swords, begin to fight. But just as Raoul finds himself overpowered a loud shout is heard: the 'cavalry' arrives, in the shape of Huguenot reinforcements. At a signal from the stage manager Catholics and Huguenots hurl themselves at each other with such unrestrained ferocity that British soccer hooligans would be put to shame.

At the height of the fighting the Queen suddenly appears and pleads with both sides to forget their religious differences. De Nevers enters and with words of affection conducts his reluctant bride to his fashionable *pied-à-*

*terre* in downtown Paris. The Queen then tells Raoul that Valentine's visit to de Nevers' chateau was to ask to be released from her marriage vows so that she could marry Raoul. Our hero realises, too late, that the woman who had saved his life and who truly loves him is the one he had so cruelly rejected. *Que les hommes sont bêtes!*

### Act 4. De Nevers' home in Paris.
It is the night of 24 August 1572, known in history as the infamous Massacre of Saint Bartholomew. A dejected Valentine is reclining on a *chaise longue* in her apartment. Like many a newly-wedded bride she is feeling somewhat disillusioned about the joys of married life and tells us about it in a boring aria that in most productions is omitted.

She turns to find Raoul inside the room: how he managed to enter undetected is known only to the producer. He has come to bid Valentine *adieu,* but on hearing footsteps approaching quickly hides behind a tapestry. He declines the *chaise longue,* remembering what happened to Cherubino in similar circumstances.

St Bris, de Nevers and other Catholics enter. Tonight, declares the fanatical St Bris, will see the end of these accursed Huguenots: when the great bell of St Germain begins to toll, their massacre will start. His announcement is greeted with cries of fervour except for de Nevers, who refuses to take part in such a bloody deed. St Bris accordingly places his son-in-law under arrest until the next day.

Next is the celebrated *Bénédiction des poignards*. Three monks enter and distribute white armbands to the conspirators. This, the producer's idea, allows them to recognise each other and thus avoid a repetition of the previous night's *débâcle* when some overzealous Catholics unwittingly slew several of their own. Then, led by St Bris, the conspirators proudly hold out their *accoutrements* to be piously blessed by the monks. This is accompanied by alternating *fortissimo* and *pianissimo chords* from the orchestra, according to the size of *accoutrement* displayed.

The conspirators leave and Raoul emerges from behind the tapestry. Horrified by the terrible danger threatening the Huguenots, his first thought is to rush away and warn them: every second counts. But just as he is about to leave Valentine drops her first bombshell: she confesses she loves him. *Quelle surprise!* Our hero, delighted at the revelation and for the chance to show off some applause-catching high notes, forgets his noble cause and instead joins Valentine in one of the longest love duets in all opera, sacrificing not only umpteen valuable minutes but untold Huguenot lives.

Suddenly the bell of St Germain starts tolling its signal of death: the massacre has begun! Flames can already be seen while the clash of steel becomes louder. Action is required. Raoul tears himself away from Valentine's arms and dashing to the open window jumps *Tosca* fashion into the street below. As he does so a shot rings out: Raoul *est mort!* Valentine lets out a scream and the curtain falls.

Or at least, that's what happens in the 4 act version. In the original 5 act version, the final scene takes place in a churchyard the same night. Raoul, badly wounded, is being helped by Marcel. Valentine hurriedly enters and offers them white armbands to save themselves, but they refuse. She then drops her second bombshell: de Nevers has been killed in the fighting and she is now free to marry Raoul. As proof of her love she will adopt the Huguenot faith, whereupon Marcel blesses the happy couple.

St Bris and his followers emerge. Seeing a group of fugitives without white armbands St Bris challenges them. *"Qui va là?"* he demands, his musket raised. *"Huguenots!"* comes the defiant reply. Three shots ring out: Too late the horrified St Bris discovers he's killed his own daughter.

# Lohengrin

Opera in 3 acts by Richard Wagner.
First produced Weimar 1850

| | |
|---|---|
| Henry the Fouler, King of Germany | bass |
| Frederick of Telramund, Count of Brabant | baritone |
| Ortrud, his wife | mezzo |
| Elsa of Brabant | soprano |
| Lohengrin, the Unnamed Knight | tenor |
| A herald, noblemen, noblewomen, pages etc | |

Scene: Antwerp            Time: 10$^{th}$ century

*Act 1. A meadow by the river Scheldt.*
The German king Henry the Fouler, so called because of his foul language, has come to Belgium to fight Hungary. Ach, you may ask, why does a German king come to Belgium to fight Hungary? No one knows, but Wagnerian scholars believe it's because the Hungarians have been dumping vast quantities of cheap paprika in Brabant and this has made the Belgians see red.

Telramund tells the king that Elsa, the somewhat scatty daughter of the Duke of Brabant, allegedly murdered her brother Gottfried in order to claim the throne. Telramund rejected Elsa and married Ortrud, daughter of the Prince of Friedegg. To settle the dispute the king decrees that a trial by combat be held between Telramund and whoever offers himself as Elsa's champion. Elsa then describes a dream she has had in which a knight in shining armour appeared and offered to be her champion.

A herald issues a decree for the champion to appear and before you can say *Oberbundeseignungsprüfungskommissionsausschussvorsitzender-stellvortreter* a loud quack-quack is heard from the river and a swan appears. The swan is drawing a boat and in the boat there stands: yes, you've guessed it, Elsa's knight in shining armour. Later we learn that he is standing, not to admire the view, but because he can't sit down in his armour. As the boat draws up to the river bank the knight, with a stately flourish, prepares to land. The perils of the opera house being what they are the stagehand pulling the swan accidentally gives the wire a sudden tug and the knight is jerked upwards into the air, landing flat on his face in the mud. "The knight's really in the Scheldt" is Henry the Fouler's remark.

Picking himself up with as much dignity as he can muster – no easy task when you're wearing a suit of armour – the knight sings his Farewell to the Swan, reminding it to return in act 3. He then promises to champion Elsa and even to marry her, on condition that she never asks his name or where he's from. The overjoyed bride-to-be, who's been desperately seeking a husband, eagerly agrees. What bride wouldn't? The combat between Telramund and the Knight-Who-Won't-Give-His-Name now ensues, with the latter sparing his rival's life.

*Act 2. The castle of Antwerp.*
Telramund has been banished from Brabant for slandering Elsa and blames Ortrud but she merely tells him to belt up and listen to her plan. When tomorrow's bridal procession reaches the steps of the cathedral, Telramund is to accuse the Unknown Knight of sorcery, while Ortrud, having planted the seeds of distrust in Elsa's mind, will get her to reveal her hubby's name. Ortrud could, of course, simply get his name from the libretto, but she likes to do things her way.

Just then Elsa appears on her balcony. Ortrud asks her whether she is doing the Right Thing by marrying this mysterious stranger who refuses to give his name. What does Elsa know about him? where is he from? is he tenor or bass?  From Elsa's troubled brow it's obvious that the Seeds of Doubt are beginning to bear fruit. Then playing her trump card Ortrud poses her last question: the knight may well have proved himself valiant in combat, but what if, on the wedding-night, etc etc.  Ortrud takes her leave and poor Elsa is now left more confused than ever.

Dawn breaks and Elsa's bridal procession enters. Ach, you may ask, why hold a  wedding ceremony at dawn? No one knows, but Wagnerian scholars have discovered that weddings held in Antwerp before 5am qualify for a 50% discount. As Elsa is about to enter the cathedral Ortrud blocks her way: no mean feat when you consider the cathedral portals measure nine feet across. Then Telramund, following the plan, accuses the Unknown Knight of sorcery but the king intervenes and Telramund is driven away. As the loving couple enter the cathedral Elsa assures hubby-to-be that she trusts him but the menacing figure of Ortrud pointing a defiant finger at her causes the seeds of doubt to return.


Act 3.
Scene 1: The nuptial bedchamber.
Elsa and the Unnamed Knight, now married, enter slowly.  Like all newly-weds, they are somewhat shy at finding themselves alone in a bedroom for the first time but such is the power of Wagner's love-music that before you can say *Zusammengehöigkeitsnationalgefühlsduselei*  they passionately declare their love for each other. Unfortunately the ensuing love duet is so long that by the time they've performed it they've got no strength left to perform anything else.

By now, the blushing bride is once more assailed by her Doubts. Try as she may she just cannot restrain her curiosity about hubby's identity.  In desperation she tries focusing her thoughts on happy times to come - it's her wedding-night, after all – but Ortrud's evil tongue has done its work. No longer able to resist, Elsa asks hubby the Fatal Question, but before he can reply there comes a dramatic interruption.  Telramund and four knights, having concealed themselves in the bedroom during the interval, rush in with swords drawn, expecting the Unknown Knight to be caught with his – er guard down. But having been tipped off in advance by a stagehand, the knight quickly draws his sword and fells Telramund with a single blow, thus adding another late knight to the list.

*Scene 2: Back in the meadow.*
The Unknown Knight arrives to bid the king and court farewell: Elsa having broken her promise he can now reveal all. In a famous aria he relates how he helps those in distress, usually damsels, and with *Mission Accomplished* it's time to return to those distant lands. "My father" he proclaims proudly, "is Parsifal, who runs the show. My name is...Lohengrin". "With a name like that" observes Henry the Fouler, "it's no wonder he wants it kept secret". Putting two fingers in his mouth the knight emits a piercing whistle and the swan appears, drawing behind it the same boat with which it arrived. Our hero, with a sad glance at his unravished bride, enters.

Just then Ortrud pitches up. Pointing at the boat, she announces that the swan is Elsa's brother Gottfried, whom she had changed into that aquatic bird some time earlier. A white dove appears and, hovering over the boat, decides to drop its load, narrowly missing the stage manager in the process. The knight, bidding Elsa a sad farewell, steps into the boat to sail away forever.

And with any other composer, that would be the end of the opera. But the composer is Richard Wagner and before the audience can leave it is made to sit through one of those corny Transformation Scenes without which no Wagnerian opera is complete. As the dove swoops down over the boat the swan sinks slowly into the water: in its place Gottfried miraculously rises. Elsa obligingly expires on the spot and knight and swan depart. Likewise the audience.

# *Lubbo M*

Opera in 4 acts by Giacomo Puccini. First produced Turin 1896

| | |
|---|---|
| Rodolfo, a penniless poet | tenor |
| Marcello, a penniless painter | baritone |
| Schaunard, a penniless musician | baritone |
| Colline, a penniless philosopher | bass |
| Mimi, a penniless midinette | soprano |
| Musetta, …penniless | soprano |
| Benoit, a landlord | bass |

Students, street vendors, soldiers etc

Scene: Paris                    Time: 1830

*Act 1. A garret*
It's Christmas Eve in the Latin Quarter and the great Fuel Crisis is on. High up in their icy cold attic off the Boul' Mich Rodolfo and Marcello are trying to keep themselves warm. At the window, Rodolfo is watching the busy little birds in the street below picking up what they can before Christmas. Many of them, he says, are foreign birds, returning to Paris each year and are easily recognisable by their brightly coloured plumage, rich fur and high heels.

Marcello is busy 'recycling' his picture, an unrecognised masterpiece titled 'The Passage of the Red Sea". It is dutifully sent to the Academy every year and is dutifully rejected by the jury every year. After further contemplation he 'recycles' the picture by the simple expedient of turning it upside down and retitling it "Sunset over Suez".

The temperature now at freezing point Rodolfo decides to sacrifice his unrecognised masterpiece. Picking up his play *Le Vengeur*, he stuffs the pages of its first act into the stove which with some coaxing finally produces a little heat. "A scorching success" is Rodolfo's wry comment as he watches the flames devour the pages – the only time in the play's history that it has not been refused.

Colline the philosopher enters. Extracting from his bulging pockets various books likewise extracted from various bookstalls which he then tried to pawn, he tosses them into the stove. The three Bohemians gratefully warm their hands as the stove tries desperately to give out more heat.

Schaunard appears, laden with food, drink and cash and the table is immediately set for a slap-up dinner. An unwelcome knock at the door silences their jubilation: it is Benoit the landlord, come to claim last year's rent. He enters and by plying him liberally with wine they get him to boast of his conquests. "Psst!" whispers Marcello in his ear. "I'm not!" retorts the old roué imbibing another glass of Bordeaux. Pretending to be shocked by his amorous escapades they hustle him out of the door.

It is now decided to celebrate Christmas Eve at the Café Momus, their favourite haunt. All leave except Rodolfo, who says he must first finish an article for a journal. As he begins to write there comes a timid knocking on the door. Opening it he sees it is a neighbour, a frail little seamstress called Mimi who, if we are to believe the libretto, lives on the floor above without once ever meeting him. She explains her candle has gone out but exhausted by the climb and by fits of coughing, she totters into the room and collapses onto a chair. Rodolfo, in his excitement to revive her, sprinkles some red wine over her face and give her cold water to sip.

At a sign from the prompter Mimi drops her key and she and Rodolfo search for it in the dark. He finds it, pockets it and then finds her hand, his cue for the famous aria 'Your tiny hand is frozen, let me warm it in the fire". Then Mimi in her aria tells Rodolfo that her name is Lucia but the printer got it wrong at the first performance and now it's stuck. The two lovers next sing a love duet, the final phrase of which, if sung *pianissimo perdendosi* as written, is an exquisite moment in the opera. In practice, however, this rarely occurs, because the tenor will ruin it completely by interpolating a *fortissimo C in alt* in an attempt to keep up with the soprano.

*Act 2. The Café Momus*
Despite the sub-zero temperature the Bohemians are seated outside the café. Rodolfo joins his companions and introduces Mimi, who is wearing a pink ear-muff to keep out the noise from the street. A commotion is heard offstage and Musetta enters. Best described as 'A Heart of Gold in a Tart of Old' Musetta is at various times reckless, penniless and occasionally bra-less. She is an old flame of Marcello's and it's no coincidence that the flame is at its highest when Marcello has money. The painter being broke at the moment Musetta has turned her attentions to Oliodoro, a rich oil broker, who accompanies her to a table.

Having seated herself, Musetta tries to attract Marcello's attention by various means, but he pretends to ignore her. Exasperated by his seeming indifference, she gets up from her chair and on the pretext that her back is hurting her, brazenly takes off her bra, revealing herself in all her titivating glory. *"A Triumph!"* exclaims Colline admiringly, who evidently has made a study of such matters. No longer feigning indifference, Marcello asks to be tied to his chair. Musetta sends Oliodoro to buy her a new bra and rushing to Marcello flings herself into his arms. Overcome by this sudden display of bosom friendship Marcello immediately asks to be untied.

A waiter approaches with the bill which, in Bohemian fashion, is passed from one member to the other. After seven laps round the table the bill, in Bohemian fashion, remains unpaid. The problem is solved by Musetta, who simply adds it to Oliodoro's. Taking advantage of the confusion caused by a passing military band the four Bohemians and the two girls make good their escape. Oliodoro returns, to be confronted with a *"Cav & Pag"*: ie a 'double bill' to pay.

*Act 3. A tollgate*
It's two months later and still perishing cold. An official opens the tollgate and people pass through, among them Mimi. A prolonged fit of coughing tells us that despite a government health warning she's been smoking again.

Mimi has come to find Marcello who, by a strange coincidence, now emerges from a nearby tavern. He tells Mimi he and Musetta are working at the tavern, he as painter and she as barmaid. Neither job pays very much but it allows Marcello to keep an eye on his sexy girlfriend. Musetta, for her part, enjoys flirting with the male customers, having always preferred men to liquor.

Mimi tells Marcello, between one cough and another, that she and Rodolfo are always quarrelling and that the time has come to part. He has also become madly jealous. After another fit of coughing Mimi suddenly feels the call of Nature and goes behind a nearby tree, subtly indicated in the orchestra by a pp.

Next Rodolfo appears from the tavern. How or when he arrived is known only to Puccini. He tells Marcello that Mimi is an outrageous flirt, practising low fidelity at high frequency. We also learn, as does the listening Mimi from behind the tree, that she is seriously ill and hasn't got much longer to live. Rodolfo then goes behind the tree for the same reason as Mimi but restrains himself just in time.

After Mimi sings her moving Farewell it's time for the famous quartet. Mimi and Rodolfo agree to part in the spring while Musetta and Marcello hurl endearing pet-names at each other like shop-painter, viper, toad and witch. The act closes with Mimi and Rodolfo returning to their love nest and Musetta and Marcello to the tavern where, we hear, Musetta is having a smashing time with the crockery.

*Act 4. The garret*
Still freezing so it's a case of winter drawers on. We find Rodolfo and Marcello in their garret in the Boul' Mich but without their respective girlfriends, who have left them for richer fare. Colline and Schaunard arrive and preparations are made for a lavish feast, with no expense spared. This is perhaps as well since, in typical Bohemian fashion, the feast is fictitious.

A knock on the door interrupts their horseplay. Musetta enters and tells them Mimi is too weak to climb the stairs. Rodolfo and Marcello bring her in and gently lead her towards the bed. Musetta and Marcello then leave together. Colline prepares to take off his coat in readiness for his Coat Song but finding the sleeves have been sewn up is obliged to sing his aria still wearing it. He stalks out in a fearful temper vowing to beat up whoever played the trick on him. Later he discovers it was done by Caruso many years earlier but being an old production no one had bothered to check it out.

The two lovers are now alone. They talk about their past happiness but poor Mimi becomes weaker. The others return with some medicine but it is too late: Mimi is dead. Rodolfo bursts out sobbing over her body and the curtain falls.

# *Macbeth*

Opera in 4 acts by Giuseppe Verdi.
First produced Florence 1847

| | |
|---|---|
| Macbeth, an army general | baritone |
| Lady Macbeth, a chronic alcoholic | soprano |
| Macduff, a Scottish nobleman | tenor |
| Banquo, an army general | bass |
| Duncan, King of Scotland | mute |
| Malcolm, his son | tenor |

Witches, soldiers, servants, messengers etc.

Scene: Scotland                   Time: 11$^{th}$ century

*Act 1 Scene 1. A heath. Three groups of witches, seated round a fire, drinketh whisky while awaiting the prompter's cue to begin.*

1st group.　　We are the witches threesome, o what horrors! [*prompter waves*]
　　　　　　　ah! there's the signal for the op'ning chorers!

2nd group.　　All night we've spent in keeping constant watch,
　　　　　　　it's such a bore, so how about a scotch?

3rd group.　　More meet 'twould be to follow the libretto
　　　　　　　and give a hero's welcome to Macbetto!

*[Enter Macbeth and Banquo]*

Witches [all]　All hail, Macbeth! We greet thee Thane of Cawdor,
　　　　　　　and then as King of Scotland, in that order
　　　　　　　no battles shalt thou lose when thou art king
　　　　　　　except the very last. Watch out, old thing.

Mac *[to Banquo]*　Who can believe this weird, outlandish story?
　　　　　　　'tis madder than the plot of *Trovatore*
　*[to witches]*　your words, dear friends, seem spoken from the pulpit
　　　　　　　how do I know they're not a load of bull....?

Witches　　　Hold on, Macbeth, or you'll become a cropper
　　　　　　　here comes a chap to prove our words are proper

*[enter messenger, lisping]*
　　　　　　　Thing Duncan thends me forth without delay
　　　　　　　of Cawdor he hath named thee Thane today!

Mac　*[aside]*　Their words ring true! Success is surely mine!
　　*[to witches]*　　let's have a drink before I'm home at nine!

Witches [all]　Good luck, milord!
*[raising glasses]*here's to a special pact
　　　　　　　to meet again before the final act! *[Exeunt]*

*Scene 2. A hall in Macbeth's castle. Lady Macbeth, sipping a scotch, doth read a letter in which Macbeth describeth his meeting with the witches and their prophecy.*

Lady M.          Macbeth has struck it lucky, there's no doubt
                    but hush! These tidings mustn't get about.
                    tho' brave, Macbeth is victim of his guilt,
                    I wish he'd show more valour 'neath his kilt!
*[drains glass]* *[enter servant]*
Servant          Good news, milady! King Duncan's on his way
                    to spend the night here at our castle gay *[exit]*

Lady M *[exultantly]*   Here lies our chance to make us king and queen
                    the King must die tonight by hand unseen!
*[pours herself a gin and tonic and gazes fixedly at contents]*
                    so come you spirits, unisex me here,
                    another glass and I'll be full of cheer! *[drains glass]*

*[enter Macbeth]* Come in, my lord!
*[offering glass]*  let this thy spirits rouse
                    do what I say and Scotland will be ours.
                    King Duncan sleeps tonight beneath our roof
                    prepare thy trusty blade, don't make a goof!
                    steal in his room, and with thy dagger ready
                    give him the fatal thrust, direct and steady.

Mac  *[angrily]*  What meanest thou, o wife? What is this phooey?
                    hast thou been at the scotch or the Drambuie?
*[looks around]*  and where's that case of export gin and tonic
                    a gift from London's School of Economics!

Lady M.          Now list to me, thou weak-willed Sassenackie
                    the blame will fall on Duncan's sleeping lackey
                    his clothes with blood we'll smear from off thy blade
                    and thus upon himself will guilt be laid

Mac  *[calmer]*  So be it, then, I'll sharpen well me knife
                    at half-past twelve King Duncan ends his life.
                    but first, to give me greater strength and courage
                    pour me a scotch to drink before me porridge!

*[enter Duncan accompanied by Banquo, Macduff, Malcolm etc]*
Duncan          A hearty evening, sir! and to you, madam,
                    we've journey'd well upon your new macadam
                    these modern roads make Glasgow's look like relics
                    hast thou reserved my rooms? I sent a telex.

Lady M *[looketh meaningly at Macbeth]*
        'Tis ready, Sire, it's on the second floor
        just take the lift to chamber twenty-four
        but 'fore ye go why don't you have a candy
        and chase it up with cognac or a brandy
                *[Exeunt Duncan, Lady Macbeth, etc]*

Mac   *[alone]*  My lady said to harken well the bell
*[sees a bottle of Bell's whisky]*
        but what is this? I see another Bell!
*[drinks a glassful] [a bell soundeth]*
        aha! the bell! All seconds out the ring,
        tomorrow morn Macbeth will reign as king! *[exit]*

*[enter Lady Macbeth]*
Lady M.      Press on, Macbeth! ne'er from thy purpose swerve *[sees bottle]*
        methinks I'll have another for me nerves!
*[drains glass]*
        aha! that's good! There's nothing like a chaser
        to make you think that ev'rything looks safer!

*[enter Macbeth, horror-stricken]*
        Methought I heard a voice that pierced my heart
        cry out "Macbeth, a murderer thou art!"

Lady M.      Take back thy bloodstain'd dagger to the room
        and with it smear its blood upon the groom *[Macbeth recoils]*
        dost thou refuse? Give me the dagger, cissie,
        I'll do the job meself in half a jiffy!
*[exits but returneth soon after]*
        'Tis done, Macbeth.
        Those bloodstains came in handy,
        now let's to bed, I'm feeling rather randy
        and while the solo flute performs its coda
        let's drink to Scotland's King with scotch-and-soda!
                *[exeunt]*

*[enter Banquo and Macduff]*
 Macd.      The morn is dark, the weather foul and dirty
        I'd best awake the king, it's seven-thirty.

*[Macd. enters the room but on discovering the crime doth rush out in horror]*

                O day of woe! O wretched blow ill-fated!
                the King is dead, by unknown hand castrated!

*[The entire household is roused and doth vengeance swear on the murderers]*

All.          What hand hath done this deed, so base and fiendish,
               to slay our King, then murder the King's English?
               The punishment on him who made this hap
               is thirty days condemned to non-stop rap!

*Act 2 Scene 1. A room in Macbeth's castle. Enter Macbeth and Lady.*
Lady M.      And now, Macbeth, that we are King and Queen
               resolve thy heart, aye, harden well thy spleen,
               ignore thy troubled conscience, do not hark it
               to bump off Fleance and Banquo now's thy target

Mac.          OK, my love, but in my royal station
               I cannot risk another 'sassination
               a murder such as their's a special job
               it's best to use the experts: call the Mob!

LadyM. *[sotto voce]*    I've heard it said, my lord, there is a man
               who heads a private group known as 'The Clan'
               but tho' I've searched each Tartan's date of entry
               I cannot find this clan in *Landed Gentry*

Mac.          *Sans faire rien*, my love, as French wouldst have it
               this clan's a special group and rather tacit
               to work in secret is their dedication
               I'll pay them well to show my 'preciation! *[exeunt]*

*Scene 2. A park. Enter Banquo and Fleance.*
Banq.         I feel the evil presence here, my son
               of horrid death, so be prepared to run.
               my step is slow, my beating heart gets puffier
               if I should die, just blame it on the Mafia! *[exeunt]*

*[a scuffle is heard offstage and cries of help; Banquo is slain but Fleance doth escape]*

*Scene 3. A banquet in Macbeth's castle. Lady Macbeth, already blind drunk, raiseth her glass to the assembled guests and proposeth a toast.*
Lady M.        A toast, dear friends, to Scotland's pride and glory
                the future's looking great, all's honky-dory
                pass round the booze, a quart in ev'ry chalice
                let's drink the lot 'cos next there's only haggis!
   *[drains glass]*

*[Macbeth leaveth the banquet-table to speak to the hired assassins waiting outside. When he doth return he findeth Banquo's ghost sitting in his chair]*
Mac.            Who is this strange and ghostly apparition
                of ashen face and evil disposition?
                Begone! ne'er shake thy gory socks at me
                for 'twas not I that plung'd his knife in thee.

*[The ghost being visible only to Macbeth the shocked guests remark on his behaviour]*
Guests:        Is this the brave Macbeth who fought and conquers?
                upon my soul, he's gone stark raving bonkers!
                milady too doth find the matter risky
                just watch her gulping down her seventh whisky!
*[exeunt]*

*Act 3. A heath. Three groups of witches are seated around a cauldron of burning off-shore oil. They are reading the day's financial news and discuss the latest FTSE index.*

1st group.      Double, double, toil and trouble
                Scotland's rich through North Sea Bubble!
2nd group.     We've no need of revolution
                thanks to Britain's Devolution!
3rd group.      Stir the pot, you ugly witches,
                North Sea oil brings us riches!

*[enter Macbeth]*
Mac.            O sisters kind, of charming face and figure
                pray tell me how, before I'm mortis rigor,
                the future reads; reveal me your prediction
                just give me facts, no lies nor science fiction.

*[The witches conjureth up three apparitions. After the third one Macbeth falleth to the ground in a faint. Lady Macbeth enters hurriedly]*
Lady M.        O what is wrong, my lord? Why art thou cowed?
                here, take a sip o' golden Morning Cloud
*[gives him a glass]*

Mac *[quickly recovering]*
        My destiny's been told by these three witches
        my future plans are void and full of hitches
        try as I may I cannot beat the glitches
        I wish I'd never met such ugly bitches!

Lady M.     O list to me, my lord, this is thy mission,
        put to the sword all those in opposition
        let '*Death to all our foes!* become our motto *[producing bottle]*
        and drink this golden scotch until we're blotto! *[exeunt]*

*Act 4 Scene 1. Birnham Wood. A chorus of Scottish exiles lament their fate.*
Chorus     This opera's just a load of hurdy-gurdy
        the tunes are dull, they must be early Verdi!
        tomorrow night's another load of Blarney
        McCormack sings the lead in *Puritani!*
*[enter Malcolm]* Let ev'ry man a branch cut from these trees
        to cover up his privates, face and knees
        so when our valiant soldiers march to battle
        the sight will make the tyrant's dentures rattle! *[exeunt]*

*Scene 2. A hall in the castle. A doctor and lady-in-waiting keepeth watch outside Lady Macbeth's bedchamber; presently she emerges.*
Lady-in-waiting   But soft!
        what sound upon the night is now encroaching
        methought it was Milady's steps approaching.

Doctor     It is indeed the shuffling feet of Madam's *[he gasps]*
        beneath her gown she wears Sweet Fanny Adams!

*[Lady Macbeth, hopelessly drunk, doth slowly appear, walking in her sleep. She holdeth a lighted taper in one hand while rubbing it continually with the other]*

Lady M.     Out, out, damn'd spot! the bloody thing is stuck, sir,
*[rubbing her hands]*  I've tried Camay, petroleum and Lux, sir!
        it looks to me its found a tougher billet
        let's try a drop of methylated spirit!

*[Lady Macbeth unscreweth a hip-flask and doth try to remove the spot but fails]*
Lady M.    This sleepwalk scene reminds me of Amina's
*[takes another swig]*
I'll have to send this nightie to the cleaners
it's fun to be a chronic alcoholic
there's always time for one more gin-and-tonic!  *[exit]*

*Scene 3. The castle battlements. Macbeth, alone, broods wearily over the turn of events. A lady-in-waiting doth hurriedly enter]*
Lady-in-waiting   Milord! milord! your lady is no more
at half-past ten we found her on the floor
her eyes were closed,
her mouth and cheeks inflated
she's drunk up all your scotch and methylated!

*[Sounds of fighting are heard offstage, followed by music played by a brass band]*
Mac.    Are those the martial sounds of fife and bagpipe? *[listening intently]*
that drumroll's stolen from *The Thieving Magpipe!*   *[enter Macduff]*
fly, fly, Macduff, before I slaughter thee,
the witches said no harm can come to me!

Macd.    From mother's womb I was untimely ripp'd
so say your prayers and die – admit I've pipp'd!

*[Macduff pursueth Macbeth and doth slay him. The victorious English army, led by Banquo's ghost, doth vanquish Macbeth's followers and peace cometh to Scotland]*
Chorus    Rejoice, good friends! The hated tyrant's dead
with one fell swoop Macduff did lop his head
let's celebrate the day with scotch and bourbons
and watch old Banquo's ghost dance the Gay Gordons!

ENDS

# The Magic Flute

Opera in 2 acts by Mozart.
First produced Vienna 1791.

| | |
|---|---|
| Queen of the Night | soprano |
| Pamina, her daughter | soprano |
| Tamino, a prince | tenor |
| Papageno, a birdcatcher | baritone |
| Papagena, his sweetheart | mezzo |
| Sarastro, a high priest | bass |
| Scene: Egypt | Time: Mythical |

*Act 1. Scene 1. A rocky region. Tamino, pursued by a huge serpent, rushes on, crying for help.*
Tam        O who will save me from this awesome whammy? *[aside]*
               I daren't be late for my first date with Pammy!
               if I'm not at her place by seven-thirty
               she'll get upset and Queenie will get shirty!
*[he faints]*

*Three ladies, armed with spears, enter and slay the serpent. Gazing at the reclining figure of the unconscious prince, they comment in asides on his good looks]*
1st lady      This youth is quite a dish, I do declare
               I'll wake him with a kiss, if I should dare!

2nd lady     If I can be alone with him this night
               We'll have such fun he'll soon forget his plight!

3rd lady      I'll find a way to fox the other two
               then he'll be mine and nothing they can do!

All three     But what about the vows we duly swore?
               Our duty calls, farewell! Oh what a bore! *[exeunt]*

*Papageno, dressed like a bird and carrying a set of pipes, enters.*
Pap  I'm dressed like this because of Schikaneder
 who wrote the script and made me a bird trader
 I live on fruit and nuts and dried up barley
 I'm IQ.low and look a proper Charlie!
 *[to Tamino]* twas I who saved thee from this situation
 henceforth my name is 'Hero of the Nation!'

*The three ladies reappear carrying a padlock*
All three  Just hold thy tongue, thou brainless, birdlike creature
 this padlock on thy lips shall be thy teacher!

*They fit the padlock on his mouth and give Tamino a snapshot of Pamina.*
Tam  This Pammy's kinda cool and quite a honey
 I'll chat her up to find if she's got money
 the daughter of a queen should be quite wealthy
 her gold will make my bank account more healthy!

*The Queen of the Night enters, accompanied by her three ladies.*
Queen  Here lies me chance to advance all me plans *[aside]*
 and get unmarried daughter off me hands! *[addressing Tamino]*
 Proceed at once, go to Sarastro's palace
 and free my daughter from his evil malice!

*The three ladies remove Papageno's padlock and instruct him to accompany Tamino on his mission. Tamino is given a magic flute while Papageno receives a set of magic bells.*


Scene 2. *Sarastro's palace. Pamina is held captive by Monostatos, a Moor who, at the sight of Papageno, flees in terror. Papageno tells Pamina about Tamino.*

Pap  A noble prince thy portrait hath enraptured
 but deeply sad to learn thou hast been captured
 he's on his way to free thee from thy sorrow
*[he sneezes loudly]*
 hast thou a tissue I could kindly borrow?

Pam             Thy words bring comfort to my aching heart
                I love the prince and we shall never part
                for love that's true doth make the world go round
                and when we're wed our happiness is crowned

*Scene 3. Tamino is undergoing his first test and has been brought to a grove with three temples. He tries to enter the first two but is ordered back; at the third temple the door is opened by a grumpy old priest, evidently angry at being disturbed.*

Priest           What brings you, fearless stranger, to this door
                 and tell me what the hell you're looking for
                 I'm busy watching Liverpool play Chelsea
                 so kindly tell me why you've come to see me
Tam              I've come to find Pamina, Queenie's daughter
                 the heroine of Mozart's *Zauberflöte*
                 Sarastro stole her from her mother's care
                 the tyrant then installed her in his lair!

Priest           You are deceived, o youth, this information
                 Is up the spout, this is the situation:
                 Sarastro took the girl, not any other
                 because he had to save her from her mother!

*[A chorus from within confirms that Pamina is alive. As Tamino joyfully plays his magic flute, wild animals emerge and lie at his feet enchanted by the sound. Pamina and Papageno escape from the palace but are captured by Monostatos and his slaves. Papageno plays his magic bells causing his captors to happily dance].*
Slaves           These magic bells our feet and fingers tingle
                 it's much more fun than watching TV jingles!
                         *[Enter Sarastro]*
Chorus           Long live our mighty leader, great Sarastro
                 for symphony or opera he's a maestro!

Pam  *[kneeling]*O Mighty Lord, I humbly crave thy pardon
                 forgive my flight, thy noble heart unharden
                 I fled thy court because of Monostatos
                 I love the prince so pray thee, do not part us!

*Monostatos brings in Tamino and the two lovers meet for the first time. They embrace but are separated and are led away to undergo new trials.*

*Act 2. Scene1. Tamino and Papageno are to undergo their second trial, this time of silence.*

Sarastro         To pass this test you've gotta be quite mute
                     but are allowed to play your magic flute
                     for Papageno it's a tougher nut
                     that mouth of yours: you've gotta keep it shut!

Tam              The stakes are high but I shall try my best
                     to win Pamina and to pass the test
                     but where's me faithful mate ol' Papageno?
                     I heard him playing pipes *a poco meno*

*Papageno appears and the two begin their trial of silence. The three ladies enter and try to entice them back to the Queen's realm but they resist. The Queen herself enters angrily.*

Queen           'Tis time I had revenge, and I shall take it *[aside]*
                     I've four top Fs to sing, I'll have to fake it!
                     I ain't so young no more, a single mother
                     Why Mozart wrote these notes I'll ne'er discover!

*Scene 2. Papageno meets an old crone who tells him she is 18 years old but before she can reveal her name there is a clap of thunder and she disappears.*

*Scene 3. Pamina, heartbroken at Tamino's silence towards her, contemplates suicide.*

Pam             Tamino speaketh not, no longer loves me
                     However much I try he just won't have me *[takes dagger]*
                     In Egypt here I am like poor like Aida
                     a princess just like me, no one to save her!

*As she is about to plunge the dagger into herself three genii appear and snatch it from her. Tamino still loves her, they say, but is bound by his oath of silence not to speak. They take her to him and together they pass the final test and are finally united.*

*Meanwhile, Papageno breaks his oath of silence and chats to the old woman who reappears.*

Woman        Give me thy hand, my dearest
            *[aside ]* This ain't *Là ci darem*
                    but if these words thou fearest
                    then to prison thou art in!

*Papageno takes her hand. She is instantly transformed into a beautiful young girl called Papagena but is immediately whisked away. In the next scene Papageno, deprived of his sweetheart, takes a rope to hang himself.*

Pap            Methinks the time has come to end me life
I've no more birds to catch, I have no wife
This piece of rope I'll take and with it tether
a noose around my neck: farewell forever!

*[He looks around hopefully to see if anyone comes to rescue him]*

I'll try again. This tree shall be me gallows
With one fell swoop I'll banish all me sorrows
since no one comes to help me or to save me
I might as well go quickly to me grave-y!

*[Again no one comes to his rescue. With a final sigh he tightens the noose round his neck]*

This time I'll put an end to useless livin'
and hope my tragic fate will be forgiven
if I could only see my Papagena
compared to me she's smart and truly saner!

*He is saved by the three genii who tell him that if he plays his magic bells Papagena will be his. He does so and she immediately returns. The Queen of the Night and her three ladies enter but are vanquished by Sarastro and sink into the earth. The stage is bathed in sunlight and the opera closes with a hymn praising the triumph of Good over Evil.*

# *Manon*

Opera in 5 acts by Jules Massenet.
First produced Paris 1884

| | |
|---|---|
| Manon Lescaut, a bright young thing | soprano |
| Lescaut, her cousin | baritone |
| Chevalier des Grieux, her lover | tenor |
| Count des Grieux *père*, his father | bass |
| Guillot de Morfontaine, an old roué | baritone |
| De Brétigny, a nobleman *très riche* | baritone |

Soldiers, guardsmen, populance etc

Scene: France                    Time: 1821

*Act 1. A courtyard of an inn.*
"My name, monsieur, is Lescaut, and if you will allow me, I will tell you *l'histoire* of my beautiful cousin Manon, her rise to wealth and fame and her sad ending.

It all began in the town of Amiens. I had gone there, *vous comprenez,* to meet Manon, whose family were sending her to a convent. While waiting in the courtyard for the coach to arrive I saw two men, the *riche* Guillot de Morfontaine, Minister of Finance and an old lecher, and de Brétigny, a *riche* nobleman. With them were three very attractive, young – *eh bien,* let's call them actresses.

The coach arrives and out steps my cousin, looking *très chic* and excited. I compliment her on her beauty and she tells me it is the first time she has travelled anywhere. While I am seeing to her luggage Guillot catches sight of her. He tells her he is rich and can give her anything she wants; he even puts his private carriage at her disposal, but she knows what he's after and laughs. When I return I tell her to beware of men and then leave to join friends for a game of cards. Manon is left alone.

And it is then that the chevalier des Grieux enters. When he sees Manon it is love at first sight. He ardently declares his love and my cousin's heart is touched. She tells him she is only sixteen and on her way to a convent to become a nun.  The chevalier cries out against such cruelty.  Such beauty, he says, eyeing her trim figure and other charms, should be put – how you say? – to better use, and Manon, with a blush, modestly agrees.

Just then Guillot's postilion and carriage appear and the two lovers decide to flee together to Paris.  I return from my gambling to find my cousin missing.  *Sacre bleu!* Having had a few drinks I accuse Guillot of abducting her but monsieur the innkeeper assures me that although she left in Guillot's carriage it was with a young man.  The crowd laughs but Guillot vows he will be avenged.

*Act 2. An apartment in Paris.*
Some weeks later.  The two lovers are living quietly together in a one-room apartment in Paris.  One day de Brétigny and I decide to call on them.  We learn that des Grieux has written to his father seeking permission to marry Manon but has not yet posted the letter.  While I ask him about his intentions de Brétigny quietly draws Manon aside. A life of poverty is not for her, he says: she deserves everything that is beautiful in life and he, de Brétigny, is willing to provide it in return for – *alors, mon ami,* you know what.  He also tells her that the chevalier's father, angry at his son's behaviour, has arranged for him to be abducted that same evening, so how about it, *chérie?*

Manon, seeing opening before her a world filled with luxury and jewels, is unable to resist and accepts.  After we leave the two lovers sit down to a sumptuous dinner of *croutes de fromage* washed down by a bottle of vintage *Eau de Rubinet*.  Des Grieux goes out to post his letter.  Manon sings a sad farewell to the kitchen table, this being the only piece of furniture they possess, apart from two chairs and a bed.

Des Grieux returns and tells her about a dream he has had.  There is a loud knock on the door and as he opens it there come sounds of a scuffle followed by someone shouting *"Merde alors!"* and then silence.  As the curtain falls Manon begins to prepare for her new life 'under' de Brétigny.

*Act 3 Scene 1. The Cours-la-Reine.*
Here we are, monsieur, at Cours-la-Reine, where all Paris is out enjoying itself. Manon makes a grand entrance in fine style as all eyes turn towards her. Life under de Brétigny, she admits, has brought her everything she could ever desire: wealth, luxury, beauty.  She has also discovered that much can be achieved in life by simply obeying and taking things lying down (aria: *Obéissons quand leur voix appelle*)

Next to appear is des Grieux *père*. He tells de Brétigny that his son is about to enter the seminary of St Sulpice to take holy orders. Manon, overhearing their conversation, is filled with curiosity about her former lover and decides to see him again. Summoning her carriage she leaves *toute suite* for St Sulpice.

Scene 2. St Sulpice
An ante-room in the seminary. The abbé des Grieux has just delivered his first sermon. The congregation, consisting of *grandes dames,* are so moved by his oration that there is hardly a dry seat in the house. Des Grieux tells his father that he has decided to bury himself in the bosom of the Church in exchange for the bosom he previously used.

*Père* leaves and Manon appears. At first des Grieux refuses to listen to her but such is her fatal charm that his love for her floods back. With a cry of *"Manon!"* he takes her in his arms and is not displeased to feel that the bosom he thought was dead is, *au contraire,* very much alive and throbbing against him. Throwing away his monk's habit he resumes a former habit which Manon greets rapturously as the curtain falls.

Act 4. The Hotel de Transylvanie.
The hottest number on the Paris circuit. Fierce gambling is in progress. Guillot and his actresses are already there. I learn that due to Manon's extravagances the chevalier is almost broke. Guillot challenges him and des Grieux, staking all he has, wins again and again. Seeing a chance to get his revenge on Manon Guillot falsely accuses des Grieux of cheating and calls the police. Manon and des Grieux are arrested: he is taken to prison, while she is taken to an institution reserved for those ladies of cheerful disposition but dubious character.

Act 5. The road to Havre.
And so, monsieur, we come to the last act in my *histoire de Manon.* My poor cousin, together with a bunch of *filles publiques,* is to be deported to Louisiana. Des Grieux, who has been freed, hopes to get Manon released and asks my help. Along the road to Havre we meet the wretched convoy of women escorted by soldiers and by bribing the sergeant in charge I succeed in having Manon released for a while. The poor girl is already half dead from exhaustion and is unable to walk any further. The two lovers sing of their past happiness but Manon's strength has gone and with an anguished cry of *"Et c'est l'histoire de Manon!"* she falls to the ground and expires.

And that, monsieur, is the story of Manon. Thank you for listening.

# The Marriage of Figaro

Comic opera in 4 acts and 2 bedrooms by Mozart.
First produced Vienna 1786

| | |
|---|---|
| Count Almaviva, grandee of Spain | baritone |
| Countess Rosina, his wife | soprano |
| Figaro, his valet | baritone |
| Susanna, the Countess's maid | soprano |
| Cherubino, a page | mezzo |
| Marcellina, a housekeeper | mezzo |
| Doctor Bartolo, a physician | bass |
| Don Basilio, a music teacher | tenor |
| Antonio, a gardener | bass |
| Barberina, his daughter | soprano |
| Servants, peasants, etc | |

Scene: Almaviva's castle near Seville        Time: 18$^{th}$ century

*Act 1. Figaro's bedroom*
" A few years, señor, have passed since we last met, so let me bring you up to date. I was then a barber. Count Almaviva married the fair Rosina, I became his valet and the couple are now living on the Count's estate near Seville. But after a few years the Count has tired of marriage and is casting his roving eye again. He has become arrogant and bad-tempered, while as a result of his sexual excesses his voice has dropped from tenor to baritone.

After the dashing overture, Susana and I are shown in our bedroom adjoining the Count's apartment. It's our wedding-day, and in accordance with an ancient marriage-custom Susanna is trying on her bridal outfit before we put our things together on the wedding-night. "Now that I'm closer to my master" I tell her, "I'll be in a position to serve him better". "Yes" rejoins Susanna pointedly, "and while you're away, he'll get *me* in a position to serve *him* better!" and she explains that the Count, having tired of chasing outside game, has turned his amorous attentions to her: it's not for nothing he's called *Almaviva* (Lively Soul).

At this, I remind Susanna of the Count's official renunciation of another ancient custom, the hated *Droit du Seigneur,* which the girls on his estate, on their wedding-night, were obliged to accept lying down. But despite his renunciation, says Susanna, the Count is still determined to obtain the goods, albeit by other means. ¡*Muy bien!* I say to myself, I'll show this little count a thing or two, and in my aria *Se vuol ballare, signor contino,* I vow to beat him at his own game.

Old Marcellina and Doctor Bartolo enter. I should explain, señor, that because I owe Marcellina a few pesetas, I had rashly promised to marry her if I couldn't repay the debt. As luck would have it, that old battleaxe of a housekeeper has chosen this very day to charge me with breach of promise, aided and abetted by that cantankerous Bartolo, who has never forgiven me for having snatched away Rosina whom he was planning to marry for her money. These two are planning to stop my marriage to Susanna but they won't succeed, not if my name's Figaro!

Cherubino, the Count's lovesick page, enters. Like Siebel in *Faust,* Cherubino is really a girl in disguise. This uncertainty about his true sex is expressed in his aria *Non so piu cosa son,* or "I no longer know what I am". Cherubino has come to Susanna for a ribbon from the Countess but on hearing footsteps quickly dives behind a chair. Sure enough it's the Count. Finding Susanna alone, he begins flirting with her but on hearing footsteps approaching he hides behind the same chair as Cherubino. But the page, like Speedy Gonzales, is one move ahead. Unseen by the Count he jumps nimbly into the chair, which my quick-witted Susanna hastily covers with her bridal dress.

This time the intruder is that scandal-mongering music teacher Don Basilio. Thinking Susanna is alone, he tells her about the page's flirting with the Countess. The Count, unable to control his anger, emerges from his hiding-place and declares that the insolent page must be punished. It was only yesterday that he found him in compromising circumstances with Barberina, the gardener's daughter: that page has a habit of turning up in the most unlikely places! As if to prove his point the Count dramatically lifts the bridal dress from the chair and guess what: there is the page again!

This is too much for the Count. In a fury he orders Cherubino to leave his service immediately. But when the page 'innocently' remarks that he did his best *not* to overhear the Count's overtures to Susanna Almaviva, realising his awkward position, calms down and sulkily ponders what to do next.

And this is where I come in. Having learnt what has happened, I intercede on Cherubino's behalf and the Count, instead of dismissing him, gives him a commission in his regiment. The act closes with my singing the famous *Non piu andrai* which, it is said, Mozart 'lifted' from the last act of *Don Giovanni*.

*Act 2. The Countess's bedroom.*
This being a comedy played in and out of bedrooms, the scene changes from my bedroom to that of the Countess. We find her lamenting the loss of her husband's love, naively hoping for its return. She may well hope, señor, but with philanderers like Almaviva, there is, alas, no hope.

Cherubino enters, and in accordance with my plan the Countess and Susanna undress the page –he loves this –and disguise him as a girl. Susanna goes to fetch another ribbon but while she's away there is a sudden knock on the door: the Count demands admittance. Fearful of being discovered again, Cherubino is bundled into the dressing-room and the door is locked after him.

Full of suspicion, the Count looks around the bedroom. Who is in that dressing-room, he demands? Why is it locked? Aha, the Countess is concealing a lover!

When she refuses to unlock it, he hurries off to procure tools to force open the door, taking her with him. But he had reckoned without my clever Susanna! Having returned earlier she had hid behind a screen and springing swiftly into action, unlocks the door and changes places with the page, who quickly makes his escape by jumping out of the window.

Now begins the classic farce so beloved by the old Hollywood movies. The Count and Countess return and the latter confesses to her husband that there *is* someone in the room. The Count, triumphant, forces the door and flings it dramatically open. You should have seen his face, señor: instead of a cowering lover, out steps a smiling Susanna! What a gaffe! Completely deflated, the Count can only beg the Countess's forgiveness which she, o foolish woman, graciously grants. Will these women never learn?

My plan now seems OK until Antonio, the half-drunk gardener, arrives. He tells the Count that someone had jumped out of the window and had dropped a letter in the flower-beds. ¡caramba! more trouble! I tell the Count it was I who jumped out of the window and dropped the letter. The Count, his suspicions returning – suspecting *me*, señor, of all people – asks me what was in the letter. *Que diábolo,* I think to myself, what was in the letter? Luckily Susanna comes to the rescue: she whispers it was the page's commission which the Count had forgotten to seal and I am able to give the right answer.

Another close shave for Figaro! We all breathe freely again when there comes another glitch: Marcellina chooses this very moment to show the Count her claim on me. After making a show of examining the documents that s.o.b of a Count announces that until the claim is settled my wedding is off. There follows a squabbling septet and Susanna and I look at each other: thanks to Almaviva again we're back to square one!

*Act 3. The ballroom of the castle.*
In the third act, señor, the scene changes from bedroom to ballroom. The Count is in an ugly mood. Not only does he suspect that something is afoot, but he feels that someone is pulling his leg.

Susanna enters, and the Count immediately perks up. Seizing his chance, he begins to chat her up and this time, pretending to fall for his charm, she agrees to meet him secretly in the garden that night. Elated, the Count upbraids her for keeping him waiting so long. Susanna, still playing along, begs the Count not to hold it against her, to which he replies that *that* certainly wasn't his intention.

It is now time for the so-called legal hearing. That spiteful old windbag Marcellina has presented her case and I am called upon to defend myself. *¡Dios mios!* Now I know how poor Radames felt when facing the wrath of Ramfis and the priests!

I begin by stating that I am a gentleman by birth (loud sneers from the Count) but I was stolen when still an infant and my parentage has remained a mystery. My only proof, I continue, is a mark on my right arm, in the shape of a spatula. At these words Marcellina becomes strangely excited and after examining the mark suddenly embraces me as her little Raffaello! *Raffaello?* Si, señor: by a strange quirk of fate, I discover I am none other than Marcellina's long-lost son. She wasn't – ahem- married at the time. And my father? another bombshell: Doctor Bartolo! I am saved! Putting it politely, it appears I am – well, señor, something the Count calls me in his angrier moments.

I was so surprised at this astonishing revelation that you could have knocked me down with the proverbial. As for the Count, he was so dumbfounded he could hardly speak –'out for the count' you might say - and when he did his voice seemed to have dropped from baritone to bass! And no wonder, señor, for with the claim against me null and void he can no longer object to our marriage. Deeply humiliated, he goes into another sulk but soon brightens up: he still has the rendezvous in the garden with Susanna! As preparations for our wedding resume the Count goes off to check that his gardening equipment is in working order for tonight's job.

*Act 4. The garden.*
It is night. The garden is empty, then little Barberina appears, looking upset. And no wonder, for her first words are *L'ho perduta*, which makes me think that her relationship with Cherubino is not so innocent as was supposed. Soon after, the Countess and Susanna enter. They have a plan, of which I know nothing, of exchanging cloaks: Susanna, disguised as her mistress, hides in the garden; the Countess, disguised as Susanna, prepares for the meeting with the Count.

A moment later the Count enters. Mistaking the disguised Countess for Susanna, he ardently pours out his love of which, if she accompanies him to a nearby pavilion, he can give more visible proof. The Countess, playing along as Susanna, readily agrees. In the meantime I meet Susanna. Although I see through her disguise I don't let on, and pretending she really is the Countess I also make wild, passionate love to her until a resounding box on my ears tells me the game is over. Piqued at believing I am really making love to the Countess, she cannot restrain her feelings, but we soon make it up.

It is now time for the big showdown. Continuing my role as the Great Latrine Lover I make exaggerated love to the 'Countess' taking care, of course, to be caught by the Count, and sure enough he falls into the trap. Believing this time he really has caught his wife *in flagrante delicto* he calls the entire household to witness the 'betrayal'. While I cower away in mock terror the Count enters the pavilion to where the 'Countess' has fled, but instead of finding her there finds Cherubino, Barberina, Marcellina and Susanna!

A moment later the real Countess appears - from another pavilion! Realising what an absolute fool he has made of himself - he really is a silly count - he once more begs his wife's forgiveness and once more she magnaminously grants it. Will these women *never* learn? The opera ends with the celebration of a double wedding, Doctor Bartolo having offered to marry Marcellina! And so, señor, from me and Susanna, now my wife, ¡*Buenos nochas!*

# Martha

Romantic opera in 4 acts by Friedrich von Flotow.
First produced Vienna 1847

| | |
|---|---|
| Lady Harriet, maid of honour at court | soprano |
| Nancy, her maid | mezzo |
| Sir Tristan, her cousin | bass |
| Plunkett, a rich farmer | bass |
| Lionel, his foster-brother | tenor |

Scene: Richmond                    Time: early 18$^{th}$ century

*Act 1. Scene 1. Lady Harriet's boudoir. The beauteous Lady Harriet, the spoiled darling of Queen Anne's court, is utterly bored with court life and longs for romance and excitement.*
Lady        I find this life in English court a bore
                these gormless nerds belong to days of yore
                a dashing prince of love I'd never censure
                to bring me true romance and high adventure!

*The voices of happy, singing peasant girls are heard passing by. She asks her maid Nancy who they are and where they are going.*

Nancy      These girls, madame, are bound for Richmond fair
                it's on just for today, that's why they're there
                to be engaged for work they do aspire
                the farmers choose the ones they want to hire

Lady        Oh let's go out and join the merry throng
                disguise ourselves as servants all along
                perhaps we'll meet a handsome, wealthy farmer
                disguised like us, a knight in shining armour!

*Scene 2. Richmond fair. The sheriff reads out the rules on the hiring of servant girls.*
Sheriff       The terms of your employment are thus laid:
                "Whoever gives herself for work be paid
                a sum of money, binding for a year
                no change can then be made" – the law is clear

*Plunkett and Lionel have come to hire servant girls for their farm, but so far have found none suitable. Lionel tells Plunkett about his origins.*

Lionel          I still remember, when I was a child
                    a fugitive from justice, old and tired
                    for reasons I'm unable to discover
                    had left me in the care of your dear mother
                    he told her: should misfortune come my way
                    to hasten to the Queen without delay
                    and show Her Majesty a precious ring
                    by virtue of good fortune it would bring!

*Milady and Nancy, dressed as servant girls and escorted by Sir Tristan, arrive at the fair, where they immediately attract the attention of Lionel and Plunkett. Having heard the other servant girls reciting their skills at cooking etc Lady H offers hers as a singer.*

Lady H         Good day, kind sirs, my name is, simply, Martha
                    I've sung in Gounod's *Faust* and *Traviata*
                    this pretty lass is Julie, she's much better
                    at singing risqué songs and operetta!

*Plunkett and Lionel, delighted with their find, clinch the deal and in accordance with the law money is passed. The two girls are bundled into a wagon and taken to the farmhouse, unaware of the conditions of hire read out by the sheriff.*

*Act 2. The farmhouse. Plunkett shows the girls the kitchen and orders them to prepare supper which they indignantly refuse to do. An attempt to teach them how to use a spinning wheel also ends in failure. Martha and Lionel are left alone.*

Martha *[aside]* This Lionel is so handsome and so charming
                    his glances have a grace I find disarming
                    and tho' his clothes are like those of a peasant
                    his elegance of bearing is so pleasant!

Lionel *[aside]*   Oh ne'er have I beheld a maid so fair
                    whose beauty is so rare, beyond compare
                    such unsuspecting feelings of delight
                    will plague my heart forever, day and night!

Martha *[aside]* Not knowing just what Destiny has in store
                    I think I'll sing a song by Thomas Moore

>           von Flotow, having heard it played before
>           just 'lifted' it and put it in his score!

*She begins to sing 'The last rose of summer', much to Lionel's admiration, who joins her in the second verse. Plunkett and Nancy return as a clock strikes midnight. After wishing all goodnight the girls make their way to their quarters. Outside their room they find a waiting carriage and Sir Tristan, who takes them back to the court.*

*Act 3. A forest near Richmond. A hunt is in progress. Lady H has left it and has wandered off alone. By chance she meets Lionel but pretends not to know him.*

| | |
|---|---|
| Lionel | O Martha, dearest one, can this be you? |
| | I've searched all Richmond Park without a clue |
| | e'er since you left the farm I've felt so blue |
| | I cannot live without you, it's so true! |
| | |
| Martha | Who are you, sir? to me you're just a stranger *[aside]* |
| | this situation puts me in great danger |
| | if I should cry for help they'll come along *[she calls out]* |
| | oh joy! the hunters come, I hear their song! |

*Members of the hunt hurry to her call and surround Lionel. When he sees how Martha is respectfully treated he realises he has been duped. Angrily, he addresses the courtiers.*

| | |
|---|---|
| Lionel | This servant girl you see in rich attire |
| | is rightly mine by virtue of her hire |
| | at Richmond fair she did agree to work |
| | I never knew beneath that face would lurk |
| | a scheming mind to steal from me the gold |
| | I'd paid her in good faith; how I've been sold! |
| | |
| Martha | These words are of a madman, I profess |
| | and quite devoid of meaning, I confess |
| | I've never seen this man in all my life *[aside]* |
| | oh how I wish that I could be his wife! |

*Martha rejoins the party and returns to the hunt. Lionel remains alone, deeply hurt.*

*Act 4. Scene 1. The farmhouse. Lionel is suffering from depression. Remembering the ring he asks Plunkett to show it to the queen. Plunkett returns greatly excited.*

| | |
|---|---|
| Plunkett | That ring of yours has opened doors, my friend |
| | the court's abuzz with news, you're on the mend! |
| | the ring has proved you are the Earl of Derby |
| | so claim your rights, this ain't a load of blarney! |
| | Your grungy peasant outfit you must hide |
| | and buy some clothes that you can wear with pride |
| | at court the queen will hand you an indenture |
| | so get yourself a suit from Marks and Spencer! |

*Scene 2. Outside the farmhouse. In order to bring Lionel and Martha together again Nancy and Plunkett have recreated the scene at Richmond fair where the two first met. Plunkett takes Lionel to the 'fair', now bustling with servant girls and crowds of people.*

| | |
|---|---|
| Lionel | 'Twas Richmond fair, yes that is where I saw her |
| | what would I give, just to relive, that moment with her! |
| | I've checked on *'Missing'* websites, found no data |
| | oh where can you be now, beloved Martha! |

*[Suddenly he hears an offstage voice singing 'The last rose of summer']*

But hark, that's not a lark, that sound of greeting
that's Martha's voice, how I rejoice, my heart is beating!
a mutual flood of love is now returning
and soon a great new life for us is dawning!

| | |
|---|---|
| Martha | O speak to me again those words so tender |
| | those magic words that made my heart surrender |
| | for Cupid from his bow we two has darted |
| | to make sure you and I shall ne'er be parted! |

*[He takes Martha into his arms]*

| | |
|---|---|
| Final chorus | So ends our play, the lovers are united |
| | the queen decrees that Lionel shall be knighted |
| | and "Love doth conquer all" shall be our motto |
| | thanks to the music written by von Flotow! |

# *Die Meistersinger*

Opera in 3 acts by Richard Wagner.
First produced Munich 1868

| | |
|---|---|
| Veit Pogner, goldsmith | bass |
| Eva, his daughter | soprano |
| Walther von Stolzing, a knight | tenor |
| Hans Sachs, cobbler | bass |
| Sixtus Beckmesser, town clerk | bass-baritone |
| Townsfolk, Mastersingers etc | |

Scene: Nuremberg             Time: 16<sup>th</sup> century

*Act 1*

In Nuremberg there lived a man
Veit Pognor, kind and wealthy
he was the leader of a clan
whose businesses were healthy

His Eva was a lassie fair
her smile was warm and sunny
her face was of a beauty rare
her voice was sweet as honey

"My daughter weds the man" said he
"who meets this prime condition:
A *Meistersinger* he must be
to get through the audition"

But here an awkward snag did spring
which near to tears brought Eva
for tho' her Walther sure could sing
he was no *Meistersinger*

Next day the trial did begin
before the opposition
but when he sang his *Fanget an!*
it weakened his position

For Walther's song obeyed no rule
and so they quickly damn'd it
The reason being clear to all
no one could understand it!

"The knight has failed in the test!"
squeaked Beckmesser the Mouse
"His right is forfeit in the Fest
for me, his *Lied ist aus!*"

But Sachs the cobbler rose to say
defending Eva's suitor
"The song that we have heard today
is Music of the Future"

The town clerk countered with some wit
In tones just like a cobra's
"This music is a load of s***
the words a load of *cobblers!*"

A bitter quarrel now began
'twixt town clerk and shoemaker
in which joined members of the clan
 the grocer, tailor, baker

While some agreed that to succeed
 the song must have tradition
Hans Sachs remarked: "to hell with marks!
This singer has a mission!"

At last the meeting did adjourn
but pensive Sachs did linger
what if the knight could prove his right
to be the *Meistersinger?*

*Act 2*

It was a wondrous night in June
the stars were without number
and high above did ride the moon
while Nuremburg did slumber

Now Beckmesser this night had plann'd
to serenade fair Eva
and strumming on a rubber band
sang of his love with fever

But as he sang his dreary dirge
came sounds that made him stammer
for bangs as loud as hell did surge
 from Hans Sachs' pounding hammer

Soon noise and song awoke the throng
of townsfolk from their sleeping
and ninety strong did rush headlong
into the streets a-leaping

The townsfolk's anger quickly rose
and led to blows and brawling
The town clerk, with a bloody nose
then stopped his caterwauling!

The angry mob did quiet leave
their garments split and war-torn
until one sound the air did cleave:
the Nightwatch and his night horn.

*Act 3*

The town today is all agog
with music, joy and gladness
The cobbler, in his monologue
exclaims "*Midsummer madness!*"

Our Walther opens wide the door
and enters all elated
a dream he'd had the night before
he feels, must be related

Hans Sachs, while working at his last
of ev'ry word takes heed
and in a voice of triumph blasts
"*Das ist ein Meisterlied!*"

The two men leave the cobbler's home
it's time for the aggressor
to scout around while they are gone:
the town clerk, Herr Beckmesser

The *Meisterlied* the town clerk sees
in Sach's handwriting written
and with a cry of 'Lucky me!"
runs home as tho' half-bitten!

The scene now changes to a *Feld*
with Mastersingers present
it's here the contest will be held
to judge the best contestant

The town clerk is the first one called
and sings his stolen verses
but Walther's stanzas have him fooled
his song is met with curses

Our hero sings his *Meisterlied*
And sings it good and proper
the Mastersingers are agreed:
'The best song in the Oper!'

The shout goes up around the town
'The knight has won the title!'
and Eva proudly puts the crown
upon his head so vital

Then Pogner with a gesture bold
based on an old tradition
awards the knight a chain of gold
as pukka recognition

But then there seethed in Walther's brain
the Test and how he'd muffed it
and handing back the golden chain
told Pogner where to stuff it!

At this affront the angry Guild
went dumb with indignation
until Hans Sachs the silence fill'd
and saved the situation

*"Verachtet mir die Meister nicht!"*
Sachs tells the angry Walther
"You may have won with *'Morgenlich'*
but laws you cannot alter!"

Then smiling Eva takes the crown
from off the man she'll wed
and 'midst a cheer from all the town
it goes on Hans Sachs head!

And so with Sachs crown'd King of Song
*Die Meistersinger's* ended
If I had known it was so long
I'd never had attended!

# *Mignon*

Opera in 3 acts by Ambroise Thomas.
First produced Paris 1866

Wilhelm Meister, a rich gent                       tenor

Mignon, a poor gypsy girl                          mezzo

Lothario, a wandering singer                     bass

Philine, a sexy actress                             soprano

Giarno, a cruel gypsy                              bass

Scene: Germany and Italy                         Time: 1790

*Note: Sperata, child of a noble Italian family, has been stolen by gypsies. Her father, Count Cipriani, aka Lothario, has set out in search of her and is now in Germany.*

*Act 1. Courtyard of a German inn.*

Loth          I've journeyed far and wide to find my daughter
                I've travelled many lands and crossed much water
                a dozen years have passed since first I sought her
                I've tried the Internet but no one's bought her!

*Giarno enters with a beautiful gypsy girl (no marks for recognizing Lothario's long-lost daughter). When he orders her to dance before a crowd to earn him money Mignon refuses and he threatens her with his whip. Wilhelm, taking pity on the girl, buys her from the gypsy with a cash cheque. Mignon dances for joy and holding up the cheque sings the famous aria "Connais-tu le payee".*

*A troupe of players, among them Philine, their leading actress, arrive and enter a nearby castle where they are to perform later that night. Dazzled by Wilhelm's good looks and obvious wealth Philine plans her strategy.*

Philine [aside]  This Wilhelm's very rich, my perfect match
                        already to his wealth I feel attached
                        tonight before the show my plan I'll hatch
                        and lure him with my charms, oh what a catch!
                        here at the inn a private room I've booked
                        then once he sees my cleavage he'll be hooked!

*Act 2. Scene1. In her dressing room Philine prepares for the performance. Wilhelm and Mignon enter, the latter dressed as a pageboy. She is in love with Wilhelm and is jealous of her rival. Philine and Wilhelm leave together for the theatre. Mignon is alone.*
Mignon         Among her fancy costumes and her dresses
                  I'll find one that enhances and impresses
     *[puts one on]*
                  This daring dress is one that I must try
                  the skirt has got a split up to the thigh!

*As she admires herself in the mirror Wilhelm enters and stares at her transformation.*
Wilhelm        I can't believe my eyes, oh what a beauty
                  from simple gypsy girl to sexy cutie!
                  Alas, I have to tell her we must part *[aside]*
                  for Philine's awesome assets stole my heart!

*Scene 2. Mignon, heartbroken at Wilhelm's words, is preparing to drown herself in the castle lake. Hearing applause for Philine's performance she cries out in a jealous rage.*
Mignon         The scheming Philine from me Wilhelm's taken
                  I feel I'm like Orphelia, left forsaken
                  that actress has aroused in me such ire
                  Oh that the castle be consumed by fire!

*The half-mad Lothario, overhearing Mignon's wish, goes off to set the castle on fire.*
Loth             The gypsy girl cried out 'That castle scorch!'
                  that's music to my ears 'cause I'm a Torch!
                  it don't pay much, you need no stage attire
                  one lucifer's enough to start a fire!
                  Last week I worked on *Carmen*, just Act One
                  the factory I torched, gee, that was fun!
                  the Anti-Smoking Group paid me a pound:
                  Seville's tobacco works burnt to the ground!

*Moments later flames are seen coming from the castle. Mignon, who is inside, has fainted but is rescued by Wilhelm, who carries her to safety.*

*Act 3. Wilhelm and Lothario have brought Mignon to a castle in Italy. Lothario becomes strangely excited when he find he's back in his Cipriani palace. But the shock has been so great his mind is unhinged and he can only talk gibberish.*

Loth            I'm so confused, my way of thinking's muddled
                I hear the cost of macaroni's doubled
                they say my mind is blown but I feel dapper
                I talk such crap I think I'll be a rapper!

Mignon          It rather looks my poor old dad's gone batty
                he seems to think I'm Adelina Patti!
                and like Napoleon locked up on Elba
                his madness makes him think he's Nellie Melba!

Wilhelm *[aside]* The thought of staying on in this palazzo
                is guaranteed to also make me pazzo!
                my ties with these weird people I must sever
                with Philine's ample charms I'll stay forever!


*NOTE: For act 1 hard-up producers can use the same set as for act 1 of Manon (q.v), provided they change the French inn-signs such as Bière à la pression to Bier vom Fass, Messieurs to Herren and Dames to Damen.*

# Minnie get your gun

Cowboy opera in 3 acts by Giacomo Puccini.
First produced New York 1910

| | |
|---|---|
| Minnie, owner of the 'Polka' | soprano |
| Jack Rance, sheriff | baritone |
| Dick Johnson, alias Ramerrez, a bandit | tenor |
| Nick, bartender | tenor |
| José Castro, a bandit | bass |
| Scene: California | Time: 1849 |

*As told by Nick the bartender, who was there...*

*Act 1. The 'Polka' saloon*
"Howdee, stranger, and welcome to the 'Polka'! I'm Nick. Say, lemme git yer a slug o' booze while I tells yer 'bout our Minnie, the Gal in the Golden Vest, so called on 'count o' those two gold nuggets hid underneath her top. She was also a dame who could handle a six-shooter faster than Gary Cooper.

It wuz way back in '49, when the Gold Fever was running high. Jack Rance wuz sheriff in these parts and a mighty tough hombre he wuz too. Then there wuz Ashby, the Wells Fargo guy, me the barman and a whole crew o' reg'lar miners from the camp. The 'Polka' wuz run by Minnie, 'bout the only fem in these parts, and Jack Rance was plum crazy 'bout her.

One night, while a bunch of the boys wuz at cards, Ashby bursts in with the news that Ramerrez, a bandit with a price on his haid, had been spotted in town, but they don't pay him no attention. Jest then a row breaks out 'tween Rance and one of the miners, endin' in both men drawin' their equalisers. The situation looks mighty tense till Minnie, holster slung low and gun blazin' high, rushes in. Grabbin' the guns from outta their hands she separates the two and tells 'em to quit fightin'. All goes quiet and the men –yessir, ev'ry manjack of them – looks up to her just like a dawg looks up to his master.

The mail arrives and Ashby, openin' a dispatch, turns excitedly to Rance. "Say, sheriff" he drawls, "that road-agent Ramerrez is gonna be swingin' from a tree pronto! his ex-dame, Spanish Nina, has squealed 'bout where he's holin'up!" A crooked smile – as crooked as the sheriff himself –plays at the corner of Rance's mouth but you can see that what's grabbin' his attention right now is Minnie, 'specially those big boobs of hers. While the miners are busy readin' their letters, Rance sidles up to her and suggests the two of 'em should get hitched but Minnie tells him straight she'll only marry the man she loves. Rance goes away huffed.

A nattily-dressed stranger, a cut above the usual saloon crowd, ambles in. Sportin' a Stetson, a swell pair of Justins and the latest in Levis, the stranger goes to the bar where I serve him tarantula juice *with water* – somethin' unhoyd of in these parts! Rance starts to question the stranger, who says his name is Johnson, Dick Johnson, and that he hails from Sacramento. It seems that Minnie and Johnson have met before, 'cause when their eyes meet sparks fly. What's more, this sign of recognition don't go unnoticed by Rance, who don't like it one bit. No sir, and when some of the men start humming a waltz (not one by Johnny Strauss, 'cause he aint' writ 'em yet) and Minnie and Johnson stomp around the floor, you shoulda seen Rance's face! Shucks, that guy was so green with envy at seein' his gal dancin' in the arms of that stranger that for a minnit I thought he wuz gonna shoot up the place!

Jest then it's announced that one of Ramerrez's greasers has been captured and José Castro is brought in. When he sees Johnson he goes right up to him and whispers somethin' in his ear then, turning to the men, sez he'll lead 'em to the bandit's hideout. Led by Rance, they saddle their hosses and follow the Mex, leavin' Minnie and Johnson alone. Feelin' kinda attracted to him Minnie invites him up to her log cabin for supper so that they can palaver with no one around.

*Act 2. Minnie's cabin*
Back in her shack Minnie calls out to Wowkle, her Injun squaw, to git some vittles ready real pronto 'cause she's gotta date comin' for supper. Minnie then decks herself out in her best and waits for Johnson to arrive. Sure enough he pitches up and pretty soon he and Minnie are laughin', eatin' and drinkin' together, jest like a couple of kids. Their feelin' towards each other kinda grows and helped by Puccini's Eye-talian music they're soon in love. Minnie, who ain't never kissed a guy before, gives Johnson a big smackeroo to git the message across.

Meanwhile, a mighty pow'ful storm's abrewin' and snowdrifts start pilin' up 'gainst the door. To show she don't think Johnson is all hot hands Minnie sez he can stay the night and gives him her bed to flop in: she'll bed down on her bareskin in front of the fire. Sorry folks, that should be bearskin. Jest then there comes a mighty loud hammerin' on the door. Minnie hides Johnson behind the bed curtains and goes to see who's there: Sheriff Rance and a grim-lookin' posse have come to warn Minnie that Johnson is Ramerrez. When Minnie don't believe 'em they show her a mugshot of the wanted bandit. Sure enough, it's Johnson.

After they've gone Minnie drags Johnson out from behind the curtains. "You dirty, lowdown, double-crossin' bum!" she shouts at him, "it wuz nothin' but corral dust you done throw at me! and to think I gave you my first kiss!" Johnson, feelin' real bad, tries to explain. He admits he's Ramerrez but, he tells Minnie, since he met her his whole outlook has changed and all he wants now is to lead a decent life. But Minnie, feelin' plenty hurt at his deception, tells Johnson to take a powder. Sadly, he picks up his Stetson and makes for the door.

As he steps out a shot is fired and with a groan he falls back 'gainst the door, a slug in his gut. Minnie quickly drags him back into the cabin and somehow gits him up a ladder and into the loft. A moment later in comes sheriff Rance, a smokin' .45 in his mitt and a nasty expression on his face. "Where's that dirty Mex?" he demands gruffly. "He ain't here!" retorts Minnie, "so when you've quit nosin' around, Mr Sheriff, mebbe you'll be gittin' your thick hide outta here!"

The sheriff is jest 'bout to leave when - Holy Mackerel! - a drop of blood falls from the loft and onto his hand! "Aha!" shouts Rance, "that lousy s.o.b. is up there!" and covering Johnson with his .45 makes him come down the ladder. With the situation now desperate Minnie puts a proposition to Rance she knows will appeal to his gambler instinct. "Tell you whut, sheriff" she drawls, orl friendly-like, "let's play three rounds of poker. If you win two hands first, you take this man to the jug and me to bed; if you lose, this man is mine. And while I'm talkin' to yer, kindly take yer eyes off my boobs: they ain't yours yet!"

The sheriff, his gambling instincts aroused, figgers this is a piece of cake. Minnie cops the first hand and Rance the second. But before the third hand is dealt Minnie sez she feelin' faint and asks Rance to fetch her a drink. While he's gone she takes some cards from her stocking-top. Rance returns and shows his hand: three kings: Minnie has three aces and a pair. With a gruff "Goodnight!" Rance hightails it out and Minnie bursts into crazy laughter as she hugs Johnson.

*Act 3. The Great Californian Forest.*
In a clearin' in the forest Rance, Ashby and a bunch of guys from the camp, includin' meself, are seated 'round a fire. A big manhunt is on for this Ramerrez fellah but he seems to have given us the slip. Suddenly a shout goes up from the miners: Ramerrez has been found and dragged in.

"Hang the greaser!" the men cry out. Sheriff Rance strolls over to the prisoner and deliberately blows a mouthful of cigar smoke in his face. "Get it over pronto!" sez the bandit as the men prepare a noose. As a last request the bandit asks permission to sing 'bout Minnie. I've forgotten the toon but most folks reckon it's the only decent song in the whole opera.

Jest as they are 'bout to string him up and tighten the rope we hear the sound of gallopin' hooves and in rushes Minnie, a six-shooter in each hand. That gal had guts, man! Facing the men she reads 'em the Riot Act, tellin' 'em to spare the bandit's life - the life of the man she loves. Sheriff Rance don't like this one bit but the men, after a quick pow-wow, agree and Johnson is freed. Minnie thanks 'em all for their kindness, sez goodbye, Johnson jumps on her horse and the two lovers ride away to begin a new life together.

# Othello
## or
## Some Moor of Venice

Opera in 4 acts by Giuseppe Verdi.
First produced Milan 1887

| | |
|---|---|
| Othello, a general | tenor |
| Iago, his ensign | baritone |
| Cassio, his lieutenant | tenor |
| Rodrigo, a Venetian gent | tenor |
| Montano, ex-governor of Cyprus | bass |
| Lodovico, an ambassador | bass |
| Desdemona, Othello's wife | soprano |
| Emilia, her maidservant | mezzo |

Soldiers, sailors, townsfolk etc

Scene: Cyprus                    Time: XV century

*Act 1*
*A port in Cyprus. A violent storm doth batter Othello's ship. As it neareth port a crowd doth gather at the quayside.*

People:   Othello's ship doth madly toss and pitch
          Let's pray he reaches land without a glitch
*[The ship doth overcome the storm and safely enters port]*
          Rejoice! His ship hath braved the stormy sea
          At half past two he's just in time for tea!
*[enter Othello]*
Othello   O people hear my tidings of today
          the Turkish fleet is beaten, all's OK
          now having sung in tune my *Esultate*
          methinks I'll have a cuppa tea *con latte*
*[He drinketh of the tea offered]*

                    I thank thee, gentle people, for the tea,
                    but doth the church clock stand at ten to three?  *[Exeunt]*
Iago *[to himself]*  The mighty Moor doth loudly blow his trumpet
                    as off he goes to find his bit o' crumpet
                    here lies my chance! Avenge will I his slight
                    with Cassio here I'll start a bloody fight
*[offers wine to Cassio]*
                    Drink this, old sport, 'twill make thee gay and hearty
                    A wine that's drunk at ev'ry Gatsby party! *[to Rodrigo]*
                    Just watch the fellow drinking! Now he's missed
                    his balance at the table, how he's p*ssed!

*[Cassio, exceedingly drunk, draweth his sword and maketh to attack Rodrigo]*   'Tis clear to all his drink he's never master'd
                    another glass and he'll be properly plaster'd!
                    He wields his sword as in a game of cricket
*[howl of pain from Montano]*
                    Ye Gods! he's swiped Montano's middle wicket!
       *[aside]*    This noise and loud commotion's sure to bring
                    the Moor back from his nuptial offering

*[Re-enter Othello much angered, accompanied by Desdemona]*
Othello             What meaneth this commotion?
    *[to Cassio]*   Sir, you're p*ssed
                    Henceforth from army service you're dismissed
                    And if someone should ask you why you're sacked
                    Reply it was the Moor that had thee *blacked!*
*[to Desdemona]*
                    A hundred thousand pardons, I thee pray
                    for ne'er wouldst I disturb thee on this day
                    Boïto clearly states in the libretto
                    Othello and his bride here sing *duetto! [exeunt]*

Act 2. *A hall in the castle. Desdemona is seen in the distance.*
*[Enter Iago and Cassio]*
Iago                Good Cassio, speak thee now to Desdemona
                    and hope the Moor will grant thee a condoner
*[Cassio leaveth and doth engage Desdemona in conversation]*
                    Bravo, my friend, and now I can to all
                    reveal just how I've planned Othello's fall
                    The one who steers my course, who me created
                    Hath made me what I am, despised and hated
                    And having hatched me plot and sung me Creed
                    The Moor I'll warn of Cassio to take heed!

[enter Othello]
Othello          How now, good friend. Iago, what's the matter?
                 Hast thou some ill of which you'd like to natter?


Iago             'Tis nought, my lord, tho' troubled deep I be
[feigning indifference]
                 I like not that which over there I see

[pointing to Desdemona and Cassio talking together in the distance]

Othello [following Iago's gaze]
                 Yon Cassio chatting up me faithful spouse?
                 Wait till I get my hands upon the louse!
[violently grabbing hold of Iago]

Iago [extricating himself from Othello's grip]
                 Hang on a sec. I'll give thee ev'ry proof
                 just t'other night I slept 'neath Cassio's roof
                 and in his sleep didst hear him murmur low
                 "Desdemona, my love, let's have a go!"
                 And then, my lord, did he produce this hanky
                 which in my eyes is proof of *hanky-panky!* [aside]
                 This hanky's like a red rag to a bull
                 right o'er his eyes I"ve pulled the bleedin' wool!

Othello [beside himself with rage]
                 O that the slave had forty thousand wives
                 For each would be like forty thousand knives!
                 Iago, come! yea, kneeling in the mud,
                 doth my soul thirst for vengeance and for blood
                 Down on your knees, come, let us ring his knell
                 besides, methink it's time for *Si pel ciel!*   [exeunt]

   Act 3. The great hall of the castle. Enter Desdemona, deep in thought.
Desdem           I grieve to think of Cassio on the dole
                 with jobs so hard to find in Limassol
                 The best thing I can do to help the fellow
                 Is quickly put a word in with Othello  [enter Othello]
                 Oh husband dear, a moment, I thee pray
                 there's something I must ask thee right away
                 I've heard that gentle Cassio's got the chop
                 Won't you, my love, his execution stop?

Othello   [flaring up]

>                    Your Cassio's been dismissed and so must lump it
>                    it serves him right for chasing after crumpet
>                    and tho' I may be blowing my own trumpet
>                    I ne'er believed my wife would play base strumpet!
> *[Desdemona doth leave in tears]*
>           *[sadly]*   To think that all my hopes should come to this
>                    When but the day before our life was bliss
>                    My heart, like Canio's own, is dull and heavy
>                    God grant me strength to get through *Dio potevi!*

*[A flourish of trumpets: enter Lodovico attended by courtiers and Desdemona]*
Lodovico *[presenting letters of recall to Othello]*
>                    You are, my lord, recalled at once to Venice
>                    the singers are on strike, the crowds do menace
>                    the tenor who was cast tonight in *Marta*
>                    has left for Rome to sing in *Traviata!*

Othello *[flattered]*
>                    I do obey the Doge's high command
>                    It's nice to know my singing's in demand
>                    At half-past eight I'll finish this *Otello*
>                    by ten I'll be there sharp for Lionello!
> *[turning furiously on Desdemona]*
>                    I took thee for that punning bore of Venice
>                    who made me lose three sets at table-tennis
>                    Ye Gods! to suffer such humiliation
>                    is sure to bringeth back my constipation!
*[collapses on ground]*          *[exeunt]*
Iago *[contemptuously planting his foot on the body of the prostate Moor]*
>                    See now the Moor, so angry and half-crazéd
>                    since smutty sex its ugly head hath raiséd
>                    My evil plans have triumph'd, now I can
>                    relax and watch the refuse hit the fan!   *[exeunt]*


Act 4
*Desdemona's bedchamber.*
*Desdemona prepareth for bed, assisted by Emilia.*
Desdem       Let down me hair, dear Emmy, do not force it
>                    undo me bra and loosen me my corset
>                    for tho' I've got accustomed to its ways
>                    I much prefer the one without the stays.

                        Before you go I'll pray to the Almighty
                        And hope the Moor'll relieve me of me nightie
                        But ere I lay my head upon the pillow
                        I'll sing thee Gilbert's song about Tit Willow
*[exit Emilia]*

*[Desdemona doth retire to bed; enter Othello by a secret door]*

Othello *[gazing down at his sleeping wife]*
                        O faithless spouse, prepare to meet thy fate
                        thy sin is proved, the hour's getting late
                        for thou must die, decreed by stars ill-fated
                        as meet reward for having fornicated

Desdem *[awakening]*
                        'Twould help sir, if thy reason thou wouldst name
                        for nothing have I done to be asham'd
                        And when you've said your piece and follow'd aft
                        perhaps you'll close the door – there's quite a draught

Othello *[mad with rage]*
                        For having gone with Cassio into bed
                        is reason good enough, it may be said
                        Just now you sang an air about a willow
                        that air you'll need when stifled by this pillow!
*[he taketh the pillow and doth smother her. There is a violent hammering at the door. Emilia, in great agitation, rusheth in ]*
Emilia          What's this I see? *[to Othello]* O what a stupid clot
                        thou hast been duped by Iago's cunning plot!
                        thy wife was chaste; she lov'd but only thee
                        Upon my soul, thou art a stupid B!

Othello         Iago here didst prove how she did itch
                        To lie each night with Cassio, what a bitch!
                        Such were her thoughts, tho' one I dare not mention
                        but fornicate was clearly her intention!

Emilia          How dare thee call my mistress fair a whore
                        thou addle-pated, brainless Blackamoor!
                        To think my lovely mistress now lies dead;
                        a hundred thousand curses on thy head!

Othello         If this is true then surely I'm to blame
                        there but remains one thing to clear my name
*[he draweth a hidden dagger and doth stab himself]*

Too late, good friends! my worthless life is o'er
the deed is done: Othello is no Moor!

*[draggeth himself close to Desdemona's body]*
I kiss thy cheek, so pale and freshly-painted
I kiss thy brow, the brow I thought was tainted
I kiss thy hair, so fair and brightly lacquer'd
O stupid Moor! How truly art thou knacker'd!

*[Othello collapses to the floor beside the bed]*
And so Othello sings his last farewell
we're sure to meet in heaven or in hell
No better way to die, my love, than this,
by singing *Niun mi tema* as a *bis!*

*[Othello dieth; the curtain slowly falls]*

# *I Pagliacci*

Opera in 2 acts by Ruggero Leoncavallo.
First produced Milan 1892

| | |
|---|---|
| Canio, leader of the troupe | tenor |
| Nedda, his wife | soprano |
| Tonio, a clown | baritone |
| Peppe, member of the troupe | tenor |
| Silvio, a villager | baritone |
| Scene: Calabria | Time: 1865 |

*Act 1. Outskirts of the village of Montalto.*
*The story is told by Peppe.*

Before the action begins Tonio pokes his head through the curtains. He then sings his prologue but makes such a dreadful stecca on the high G that the public boos him.

Peppe      I see that Tonio's back from *ospedale*
               the prologue that he sang was *molto male*
               the public pelted him with old *pelati*
               not rotten ones but those *inscatolati!*

The curtain goes up showing the troupe arriving in the village. I lead the donkey cart in which Nedda is reclining; Canio beats the drum; Tonio follows behind. Canio invites the villagers to tonight's performance "a ventitre ore", or 7pm$_{(1)}$

Canio      Roll up! roll up! the show will start at seven
               we guarantee you'll be in seventh heaven
               the woes of poor Pagliaccio we unmask
               in Columbina's beauty you will bask!

(1) Canio's line has fooled many a writer on opera. It should be explained that in southern Italy it was the custom to tell the time not by a clock but by the sunset, which signified the end of a 24-hour day. As this typically occurred around 8pm it was regarded as 24 hours; 23 hours therefore corresponds to 7pm. However, many writers on opera, unaware of this local custom, continue to write 11pm, despite the absurdity of a performance starting at this time.

*Tonio goes to help Nedda out of the cart but is rudely pushed aside by the jealous Canio. Tonio goes off in a bad temper vowing revenge. A villager jokingly remarks that Tonio might be after Nedda; Canio's reply is grim.*

>That kind of game is better not to play
>whoever does will find there's hell to pay
>although the play we act on stage seems gay
>the real-life drama turns your feet to clay!

*Canio goes off to join the villagers in a tavern. Nedda, who has overheard his remarks, is fearful lest he discover her guilty secret: that she has a lover, Silvio, in the village with whom she plans to elope that night.*

Nedda  How angry were the words I heard him utter
      my heart jumps like an amp fed wow and flutter!
      my secret love he never must discover
      for if he does *'goodbye'* my Latin lover!

*Tonio enters and finding Nedda alone makes advances to her. Grabbing the whip I had thrown down earlier she slashes him across the face: for the second time he goes away vowing revenge (what with the pelati incident it's just not Tonio's day). Silvio appears. The two lovers embrace and talk of their future happiness.*

Nedda  From this accurséd place o let us flee
      this hateful, roving life is not for me
      each day a different town, a different place
      for such a life I can no longer face!

*They are seen and overheard by Tonio who, seeing a chance for revenge, hurries to the tavern to alert his padrone. As Canio returns he hears Nedda call out 'Tonight, my love, forever I am thine!" Canio gives chase but Silvio manages to escape. Canio draws his knife and threatens Nedda.*

Canio  Thy lover's name reveal, unfaithful spouse
      before my jealous rage is really roused!

Nedda  if that is how my virtue's to be tested
      then from my lips his name will ne'er be wrested!

Tonio  Don't worry, boss, you'll get your chance tonight
      her lover will be there, you'll see I'm right
      before the guilty pair prepare their flight
      just bring along your knife if there's a fight!

*It's now time to prepare for the performance. As Canio paints his face and dons his costume he sings of the clown who must laugh while his heart is breaking. At the same time, as leading tenor of the company, he thinks his fee is good enough reason to laugh all the way to the bank, hence his aria Ridi Pagliaccio!*

Canio   To people in the stalls my heart is breaking
       to colleagues on the stage they think I'm faking
       but even tho' I feel my soul is aching
       those lovely dollars show how much I'm making!

*Putting the finishing touches to his make-up he makes his way to the stage door.*
*Act 2. The same. Benches have been placed around the stage. The play begins. Nedda is Columbine, Canio is Pagliaccio, Tonio is Taddeo, Peppe is Harlequin.*

Peppe   This serenade I sing's to Columbine
       her loveliness is quite without design
       she captivates my heart, my soul entwine *[aside]*
       I hope the table's laid, it's time to dine!

*I enter the room via the window. As Columbine and I sit down to supper Taddeo bursts in with the news that Pagliaccio is coming. I escape via the window.*

Peppe   I'd best be gone, this is a danger sign
       just pour the philtre, love, into his wine!

Nedda   I cannot wait this moment so divine
       tonight, my love, forever I am thine!

*Canio, entering onstage, hears Nedda repeat the words she had spoken earlier to her lover. When he asks her who was present she replies she was alone, except for Taddeo, who is hiding in a cupboard. Canio is unable to control his feelings.*

Canio   O do not lie to me, thou two-faced diva
       how dare thee look at me, thou base deceiver!
       ten years ago I found thee in the gutter
       with nought to eat, unable words to utter!

Nedda   O bring thy flaming temper to a stop
       it's clear to all that thou hast blown thy top!

|  |  |
|---|---|
|  | if thou dost truly find me so unworthy |
|  | let me go free and no more shalt thou see me! |
| Canio | And then to fly into thy lover's arms? |
|  | no, by the gods, I'd e'er be full of qualms! |

*[pulls out knife]*

                    my heart's aflame, so stop thy clever game
                    I ask again, what is thy lover's name?

Nedda   *[defiantly]*
                    His name I'll ne'er reveal, I'll never tell
                    I'd rather I were dead, so go to hell!

*Nedda tries to escape but Canio overtakes and stabs her. With her last breath she calls out her lover's name. Silvio rushes to the stage but is also stabbed. As the knife falls from Canio's hand he announces "La commedia è finita!"*[2]

[2] In the first productions of the opera this famous line was spoken by Tonio who, it will be remembered, opened the drama with the prologue. Some years later Caruso, realising its dramatic impact, begged the composer to give it to Canio instead, with whom it remained for many years. In a Zeffirelli production at Covent Garden in 1959 the line was restored to Tonio, its rightful owner.

# *Parsifal*
## or
## the Claquers' Night Off

Comic opera *(Bühnenweihfestpiel)* in 3 acts by Richard Wagner.
First produced Bayreuth 1882

Characters in order of sanity:

| | |
|---|---|
| Gurnemanz, general dogsbody | bass |
| Amfortas, king of Monsalvat | baritone |
| Parsifal, an unknown youth | tenor |
| Kundry, an enchantress, under the spell of | soprano |
| Klingsor, an evil magician | bass |

Knights, pages, flower maidens etc

Scene: Spain and Italy          Time: Middle Ages

*Producer's note*
Like Verdi, Wagner's last work for the lyric stage was a sparkling comedy. Regarded by many as the composer's crowning achievement in the field of *Singspiel* or comic opera, *Parsifal* is in fact so highly revered that applause is strictly *verboten* lest its mystical character be profaned by the vulgar clapping of hands. This, if nothing else, proves that Wagner *did* possess a sense of humour...

*Act 1. A forest near Monsalvat Castle*
It is early morning. This is proved by the fact that when the curtain rises, the orchestral players, notorious late risers, are busy taking their places in the pit.

In a shady nook, by a babbling brook, Gurnemanz and two pages are seen at prayer. After turning over the pages, he starts preparing an outdoor bath for Amfortas, the king who had been wounded while performing a certain operation. Just then a galloping horse is heard and Kundry enters. She is described in the libretto as a 'strange, swarthy, beast-like creature, with staring eyes and smoky, dishevelled hair' a description, it is said, that Wagner based on the lead guitarist of a 60s pop group. Being the only female in this otherwise all-male cast Kundry is in constant demand at Monsalvat, serving the castle knights by day and the castle daïs by night.

Hurriedly dismounting, she hands Gurnemanz a bottle of balsam for Amfortas, who is carried in on a stretcher. Gurnemanz now relates, for the umpteenth time, how Amfortas received his wound. It seems that the king, while visiting Ravello in southern Italy, entered a magic garden belonging to a magician called Klingsor. This Klingsor had bought the castle and its garden for a song - probably the Prize Song because he got it for a low Preis - from the local government during one of its frequent financial crises. Klingsor, determined to obtain the sacred spear, had transformed Kundry into a beautiful woman, with instructions to seduce Amfortas and grab the spear.

To cut a long story short - strongly advisable, adds Gurnemanz, when dealing with Wagner's interminable librettos - Amfortas, like Tristan, had been caught *in flagrante delicto* in the magic garden. Klingsor, taking advantage of the king's vulnerable position, gave His Majesty a right royal jab with the spear. Amfortas can only be healed by being touched again with this same spear. But here's the rub: the evil Klingsor has the spear and the only person who can retrieve it, is someone described in the libretto as a 'Guileless Fool'. Accordingly, Wagner wrote this for tenor.

Suddenly a loud commotion is heard from the lake and a swan appears. The poor creature has been transfixed by an arrow and after it flops down it utters a final *quack-quack* and gently expires. Its appearance is followed by an even more curious object. An uncouth-looking youth, holding a bow and arrow in his hand and wearing an imbecile expression (no marks for recognizing the tenor) enters. When Gurnemanz accuses him of killing the swan the youth has the sulks. Gurnemanz questions him but the strange youth babbles such incoherent nonsense that Gurnemanz at first takes him for a rapper. However, it now dawns on Gurnemanz that this gawkish youth could well be the guileless fool described in the libretto and he takes him to the castle latrines for a quick wash n'brush up before presenting him to the Knights of the Holy Grail.

*Scene 2. Inside the castle*

The now cleaned-up youth has witnessed the unveiling of the Grail, a ceremony performed by the ailing Amfortas before the knights. Our hero, however, in common with the audience, soon becomes bored with the whole procedure and Gurnemanz, with a volley of curses hardly befitting a venerable old clergyman, drives him away.

*Act 2. Klingsor's magic castle*

The Guileless Fool, *aka* Parsifal, has set out to regain the sacred spear. Armed only with his innocence, his determination and a loincloth he approaches the magic castle but is spotted by the evil Klingsor on CCTV. Summoning Kundry, Klingsor transforms her again into a beautiful woman and commands her to seduce Parsifal.

The scene changes to the garden. Scantily-clad flower maidens try to entice Parsifal with honeyed words and sweet caresses, but our hero ain't havin' none of it: having attended rehearsals he knows there's better fare coming up. Sure enough, Kundry appears, looking voluptuously seductive and wearing only a few drops of perfume.

Approaching Parsifal, she speaks gently to him. Then, she takes him into her arms and pressing her mouth to his gives him a long and sensuous kiss. Our hero, forgetting for the moment his noble mission, is about to return her passionate embrace when he catches the irate eye of the conductor, whose mistress Kundry is. Deciding that discretion is the better part of Valhalla he springs to his feet and with an angry gesture casts Kundry aside.

Just then Klingsor appears on the castle battlements, sacred spear in hand. Knowing that Parsifal has come to recapture it the magician, with typical Wagnerian logic, obligingly hurls it at him. But instead of striking the intruder the spear stops halfway, suspended in mid-aria. Our hero seizes it, and before you can say *Wahrscheinlichkeitsregelbeweis-führung,* the magic castle, garden and presumably Klingsor himself collapse in ruins, leaving our hero standing in a deserted wilderness.

At this awesome spectacle Kundry falls to the ground and entreats Parsifal to save her, but our hero, with typical Wagnerian *Führerprinzip,* rudely steps over her prostrate form and clutching the sacred spear hurries away to seek Amfortas and the knights.

*Act 3 Scene 1. Back in the forest*

Some years later. Gurnemanz, now white with age, lives as a hermit. Hearing a noise from behind a bush he discovers Kundry, lifeless and dishevelled. After a quick wash n'brush up she becomes more presentable and the two await the arrival of an Unknown Visitor. A knight in black armour, bearing a spear, approaches. Yup, it's Parsifal, returning at long last. As he sits down on the grass Kundry removes his smelly socks and bathes his feet in balsam left over from act 1. She then dries his feet with her hair, the props manager having forgotten to supply a towel. When the ablutions are over Gurnemanz anoints Parsifal king and the three set off together for the castle.

*Scene 2. The castle hall*

The knights are gathered around the long-suffering Amfortas (not to mention the audience). They try to persuade him to unveil the Grail, but he refuses: a Grail warning has just come in. Uncovering his bleeding wound he begs the knights put an end to his bleeding suffering – and of the audience – by plunging their swords into him. Having put up with the king's griping for years they are sorely tempted to obey but desist.

Parsifal enters, sacred spear in hand. He touches the wound with the tip of the spear and before you can say *Mittelalterlichgeschlechtskrankheit,* Amfortas is healed 'on the spot'. The knights fall to their knees in homage and the Guileless One is proclaimed king. The curtain slowly lowers and the audience, deprived of its right to applaud, exits in silence.

# Rigoletto

Opera in 3 acts by Giuseppe Verdi.
First produced Venice 1851

| | |
|---|---|
| Rigoletto, a court jester | baritone |
| Gilda, his daughter | soprano |
| Duke of Mantova, a libertine | tenor |
| Sparafucile, an assassin | bass |
| Maddalena, his sister | mezzo |
| Count Monterone, a wronged nobleman | bass |

A page, courtiers, nobles, etc

Scene: Mantua                                Time: 16$^{th}$ century

*Act 1*
*Scene 1 The ducal palace*
The Duke of Mantova, a notorious profligate, libertine and liberty-taker, is giving an 'at home'. The great room in the palace is filled with lords and ladies, noblemen and noblewomen, cavaliers and squareheads. An antiquated stage band plays a selection of oldies, to which some old fogies practise their steps.

The Duke enters, accompanied by Borsa, head of the local Stock Exchange. "Plenty of it about" is his cynical comment as his roving eye takes in the beauties passing to and fro. He tells Borsa that his latest find is a beautiful young girl whom he has seen only in church but whose identity is unknown. He then sings *Questa o quella per me pari sono* (This one or that they're all the same to me) a ballata that sums up his attitude to women.

The stage band now begins to play a dance-hit of the '30s, ie the 1530s. The Duke, who strongly fancies the pretty Countess Ceprano, smooches up and leads her away from the dancing, much to the anger of her jealous husband. Rigoletto enters and observing what's happening waves his bauble at the Count with a rude gesture. Ceprano swears revenge.

Marullo, another courtier, now enters with some breaking news, as TV calls it: the jester has a mistress, whom he keeps hidden away in a quiet house near the palace. The courtiers, all of whom have been victims of the jester's vicious tongue, are jubilant, seeing an opportunity to get their revenge.

Their jubilation is interrupted by the dramatic entry of Count Monterone, who angrily declares that his daughter, having been seduced by the Duke, has received no satisfaction. Replying on behalf of his master Rigoletto, in tones of mock gravity, tells Monterone that the Duke too received no satisfaction from the encounter, the Count's daughter, as it were, being somewhat inexperienced in such matters. But, the jester continues, with a wink at the audience, the Duke is willing to try again, if only to live up to his motto "*After action, satisfaction*".

At this fresh outrage to his dignity Monterone's anger rises and in thunderous tones calls down curses on duke and jester. The Duke laughs it off but Rigoletto, deeply superstitious, is so moved that he is unable to move. Monterone is led away, the Duke returns to the dancing but Rigoletto remains strangely frightened.

*Scene 2. An alley outside Rigoletto's house.*

It is night. Rigoletto enters slowly, wrapped in a cloak, a hat and his thoughts. As he broods over Monterone's curse he meets Sparafucile, a professional hitman, who offers his services. "How much?" asks the jester. Sparafucile replies it depends on the hit: a VIP like a company president or a rival baritone would demand the top price; for someone of lesser intelligence, such as a popstar or a rapper, it would be less. Rigoletto replies with the customary showbiz line "We'll let you know" and the assassin slinks off, leaving behind a long, low F.

Rigoletto compares his tool with that of the assassin's: "mine is the tongue; the assassin's the dagger" (the Duke's might be called a rapier). As he arrives home he is rapturously greeted by daughter Gilda. He asks her about her movements but she replies that, unlike other girls in Mantua, she never goes to discos or nightclubs but only to church, and then – unlike the marchesa Attavanti in *Tosca*, - to pray. Rigoletto, hearing a noise, goes out to investigate, leaving the gate open for 5.75 seconds, long enough for the slippery Duke to slip in. Disguised as a poor student he tosses Giovanna, Gilda's duenna, a purse of money to shut her up and then listens in behind a tree.

Rigoletto returns and the Duke learns that the unknown girl whom he has followed from church is his jester's daughter. After Rigoletto leaves Gilda confesses to Giovanna that she rather fancies a dishy young man who follows her to church. At these words the Duke emerges and dismissing Giovanna kneels at Gilda's feet and passionately declares his love. Thrilled at finding the dishy man she loves at her feet Gilda asks his name but Giovanna hurries in with the news that she has heard voices without, that is, voices without accompaniment. Gilda quickly hustles her lover out by a side door but the two waste another precious three minutes singing a farewell duet consisting mainly of the word addio. Before leaving the Duke tells Gilda his name is Gualtier Maldé, a poor student from the London School of Economics.

As Gilda finishes *Caro nome*, the masked courtiers gather outside the house. Rigoletto returns and when Marullo tells him they are planning to carry off the Countess Ceprano he offers to help. He is blindfolded and his face masked. A courtier then climbs up a ladder, enters the house, opens the street door and carries Gilda away. In the rush she drops her scarf. Rigoletto, still holding the ladder, wonders how much longer they will be. When no one comes he tears the blindfold off and dashing into the house finds Gilda gone: only her scarf remains.

*Act 2. A salon in the ducal palace.*
The morning after the night before. In a rousing chorus the courtiers recount last night's adventures to the Duke. Learning that his bird is now within the palace, the Duke adjusts his nightcap and enters an adjoining room to 'console' her.

Rigoletto enters. Feigning indifference, he tries to discover Gilda's whereabouts. Marullo, who fancies himself as a wit, remarks that the hunchback is truly bent on finding her. A page enters with a message for the Duke but Marullo explains that he is engaged in his favourite hobby of taxidermy and can't be disturbed. Rigoletto then reveals to the courtiers that the girl they abducted is not his mistress but his daughter and entreats them to give her back. Gilda chooses this very moment to emerge from the room, her mind distraught, her hair down and her nightie up. On seeing her father she throws herself at full force into his arms.

At this dramatic moment the baritone should brace himself for the onslaught, for it could result in serious damage to his organs, vocal or otherwise. In a stern voice Rigoletto orders the courtiers to leave and Gilda relates how the Duke tricked her into believing he was only a student$_{(1)}$. As Rigoletto listens it crosses his mind that he and Monterone

---

(1) How the Duke was able to explain to Gilda his overnight metamorphosis from a poor student to the wealthy Duca di Mantova remains one of the unsolved mysteries of opera.

should celebrate Father's Day together: both are in the same situation. Monterone himself now appears, on his way to prison. Pausing in front of a portrait of the Duke and while the prompter isn't looking he spits right into the Duke's face. Rigoletto vows that Monterone will be avenged while Gilda, after her 'trying' experience in the room next door, obligingly faints.

*Act 3. An inn on the river Mincio.*
It is night. Rigoletto has brought Gilda to a squalid inn, "The *'ole in the Wall'*, so called because from outside you can see what's going on inside. It seems that Gilda is still deeply in love with the Duke and Rigoletto has brought her to the inn to show her the Duke's true character. At a sign from the prompter he tells her to look through a crack in the wall and she sees the Duke enter, this time dressed as an officer. He orders a bottle of wine and a room for the night.

This brings us to the Duke's hit-song *La donna è mobile* or 'Lady on a bicycle' as it is sometime called. It is said that that this tune became so popular after the opera's first performance in Venice that it ousted *Jailhouse Rock* from the charts. Even today, nearly 160 years later, it is still sung in washrooms and shower rooms all over the world, albeit to different words.

Sparafucile enters and thumping the ceiling with the hilt of his sword signals to his sister Maddalena to descend. Like Carmen, Maddalena knows a thing or three about men and is expert at playing 'hard-to-get'; also like Carmen, Maddalena is dressed in 'gypsy fashion', which for opera purposes means a short red skirt, a low-cut blouse and little else. The Duke, using the 'Haven't-we-met-before' technique, starts to chat her up but with a laugh she dexterously avoids his clutches. This leads to the celebrated quartet.

The quartet over, Rigoletto tells Gilda to change into male attire and then go to Verona, where she is to appear at the Arena in another performance. Inside the inn, Maddalena has fallen for the Duke's charms and can't get enough. Outside the inn, Rigoletto pays Sparafucile the first half of his forty scudi fee (duet *Venti scudi*) the balance to be paid when the Duke's body is delivered.

A storm is approaching and the Duke goes up to his room for a snooze. Taking off his sword and hat, he sings a few snatches of La donna è mobile but finding he's forgotten the tune he falls asleep instead. Maddalena, who now strongly fancies the Duke, pleads with her brother to spare his life and suggests that the hunchback be killed instead. Sparafucile indignantly refuses but eventually agrees that should anyone else turn up, he will kill him instead. Gilda, overhearing this conver-sation, resolves to sacrifice her own life and as the storm reaches its height she knocks on the door. It is opened immediately and as she enters is stabbed by the waiting assassin. Her body is then put inside a sack in readiness for the jester's return.

The storm begins to abate. As a clock strikes midnight Rigoletto emerges from the shadows and knocks on the inn door. Sparafucile drags over a sack and after receiving the remaining half of his fee (second half of duet *Venti scudi*) disappears for the rest of the opera, and not without good reason. Rigoletto, feeling pleased with himself, whistles a few bars of *Non piu andrai*, the words of which he finds suit the occasion. He drags the sack to the river bank and is just about to throw it into the Mincio when, to his horror, he hears the Duke's voice singing that abominable tune which every gondolier and errand boy in Venice has been whistling since the opera's premiere in 1851.

Feverishly opening the sack the horrified jester sees his beloved Gilda. "*É stata una fregatura!*" he cries out, and with a great cry of "*La maledizione!*" falls senseless over her prostrate body. The curse has been fulfilled.

# Romeo and Juliet

Opera in 5 acts by Charles Gounod.
First produced Paris 1867

Principal characters

| | |
|---|---|
| Count Capulet, head of the family | baritone |
| Juliet, his daughter | soprano |
| Gertrude, her nurse | mezzo |
| Romeo, a Montague | tenor |
| Friar Lawrence | bass |
| Duke of Verona | bass |

Scene: Verona            Time: 14$^{th}$ century

*Act 1. A hall in the Capulet's palace; a masked ball is in progress.*
Paris        What tidings hast thou, Tybalt, of my Julie
                I see her not within this crowd unruly
*[seeth Juliet enter with father]*
                O welcome Julie, to this festive scene
                today it is thy birthday, sweet fourteen!
                What can I bring thee from the palace bar
                a glass of chenin blanc and caviar?

Jul           Nay, nay, my lord, tonight I'd rather frolic
                I'd much prefer a double gin and tonic!
*[enter Romeo, Mercutio and other Montagues heavily masked]*

Rom       Remember, friends, this masked ball's not by Verdi
                Keep tight your masks and don't reveal your ID
*[seeth Juliet]*  Thy humble servant begs for just one wish
                to know thy gracious name – thou'rt quite a dish!

Jul           My name, o handsome youth, is Juliet
                and I'm the daughter of a Capulet

Rom  *[aside]*  What can I do? it's Murphy's Law anew
                how can I tell her I'm a Montague?

*[Romeo prepareth to leave]*

Jul  O do not leave, for parting's such sweet sorrow
    could we not meet at my place, say, tomorrow?

Rom  Tomorrow I shalt be there, beg thy pardon
    just wait for me, I'll be there in thy garden *[curtain]*

*Act 2.. Juliet's garden. Enter Romeo who standeth below her balcony.*
Rom  This song that I've prepared for voice and lute
    I've pilfered from act two of 'Magic Flute'
    *"Arise, o sun, upon this maiden shine*
    *may it bring love and help to make her mine!"*
*[Juliet doth appear on her balcony and gazeth into the garden which is in darkness]*

Jul  O Romeo, do tell me where thou art
    so I can SMS what's in my heart
    O Romeo, where art thou, is it thee? *[aside]*
    the night's so bloody dark, I cannot see!

Rom  Sweet Juliet, I'm here, stuck in the dark
    the song you heard is mine, not of a lark
    This ladder that is propp'd against the wall
    I now will climb in answer to thy call
*[As he climbeth his foot slippeth and he doth fall heavily to the ground]*

Jul  O Romeo, o swear not by the moon,
    for thou shalt then regret it pretty soon
    I simply cannot wait to see the dawning
    because we're getting married in the morning!

*Act 3 Scene 1. Friar Lawrence's cell. Enter Romeo.*
Law  Come in, dear friend, and doubly welcome be
    hast thou the score they showed on Channel Three?

Rom  I have, kind friend, and it doth make me ill
    for Man United beat us seven nil!

Law  A thousand curses be upon that team
    that dared to beat Verona's self-esteem
    but what doth bring thee to my humble lair
    hast thou some tidings thou wouldst want to share?

Rom               With Juliet I am in love, that's what
                      and she with me, our passion's running hot
                      she's on her way to ask - I clean forgot -
                      to bless us both and then to tie the knot

*[enter Juliet with nurse Gertrude]*

Jul                 Good morrow, Father, peace upon thee be
                      for Man United I'm in ecstasy!
                      *My* man united with I want to be
                       so do unite us, man, in secrecy!

Law               So be it, come, I'll now perform this mission
                      and ask thee both to kneel in this position
                      this union, I do pray, will end the strife
                      I hereupon pronounce thee man and wife

Gertrude  *[to Juliet]*  This monk, upon my soul, has dirty habits
                      he'd put to shame a colony of rabbits!

Jul                 Dispel such thoughts, o Gertie, do be sweet
                      now that I'm hitched I'm ready for my 'treat'
                      tho' Montagues are far beneath my station
                      I'm sure tonight I'll get my compensation
                      Let's close this scene by singing as a foursome
                      a great quartet that Gounod said is awesome! *[curtain]*

*Scene 2. A street. Fierce fighting between Capulets and Montagues is in progress]*
Tybalt            No mercy, friends, on curséd Montagues
                      They must all die, we have no time to lose

*[he slayeth Mercutio. Romeo enters who seeth Mercutio dead accuses Tybalt]*
Rom              O who hath done this wicked deed so base?
*[to Tybalt]*
                      I challenge thee to fight me face to face
                      I know thee for a scheming Capulet
                      the time has come to settle ev'ry debt!

*[They fight; Romeo mortally wounds Tybalt. enter the Duke]*
Duke             Such tumult and fierce fighting make me frown
                      will peace ne'er come again unto this town?

| | |
|---|---|
| Rom | Mercutio, my dearest friend, was killed |
| | by Tybalt who with hatred deep was filled |
| | this Capulet received what was his due |
| | I vowed revenge and so I ran him through |
| | |
| Duke | Thy punishment shall be thy just reward |
| | such matters can't be settled by the sword |
| | from fair Verona take thy steed and go |
| | tomorrow into exile, Romeo ! *[exeunt]* |

*Act 4. Juliet's room; enter Romeo*

| | |
|---|---|
| Rom | 'Tis time to say goodbye, my dearest wife |
| | our happiness is gone amid the strife |
| | the Duke decreed that I am to be banished |
| | and so I leave thee as a bride unravished! |
| | |
| Jul | O Romeo, I am thy wife, thy treasure |
| | we've little time, let's spend the night together |
| | when dawn doth come, 'twill give thee ample warning |
| | so let's to bed, and face life in the morning! |

*[exit Romeo; enter Capulet and Friar Lawrence]*

| | |
|---|---|
| Cap | I've come to warn thee, daughter, not to tarry |
| | it's been ordained that Paris thou shalt marry |
| | Good Lawrence here will soon perform the act |
| | So be prepared to sign the nuptial pact *[exit]* |
| | |
| Jul | O holy father, what am I to do? |
| | To Romeo I'm betroth'd, forever true |
| | |
| Law | No problem, dearest child, don't show emotion |
| | I have a plan in mind, a simple notion |
| | just drink this brew, it's quite a pleasant potion |
| | 'twill make thee sleep as if thou'rt on the ocean *[exeunt]* |

*Act 5. The tomb of the Capulets; enter Romeo who seeth the corpse of Juliet]*

| | |
|---|---|
| Rom | O Juliet! they told me thou wast here |
| | how dead thou art laid out upon this bier! |
| | my fate is sealed, this poison shall I take |
| | and so goodbye, my peace with God I'll make! |

*[drinketh poison; at the same time Juliet awaketh from her deep sleep]*

Jul    What place is this, so buried in the deep
       I see no light, this darkness makes me creep
       I hear no sound, no murmur, not a peep
*[heareth clock chiming]*
       It's half-past nine, I must have been asleep!

Rom    Sweet Juliet, I thought that thou wert dead
       stretched on this tomb to where my footsteps led
       as beautiful art thou the day we wed
       too bad we couldn't share the nuptial bed!
*[he dieth]*

Jul    Dear Romeo, farewell, our tears and laughter
       we'll share them all again in the hereafter
       there's nothing left for me to do but die
       and end my life like Madame Butterfly!
*[taking Romeo's dagger she doth stab herself]*

# Salome

*Opera in 1 act by Richard Strauss.
First produced Dresden 1905*

Principal characters

| | |
|---|---|
| Herod, Tetrarch of Judea | tenor |
| Herodias, his wife | mezzo |
| Salome, her daughter | soprano |
| Jokanaan, a prophet | baritone |
| Naraboth, a Syrian guard | short-lived tenor |

Guests, guards, loafers, gofers, etc

*Scene: Herod's palace in Galilee*         *Time: 30 AD*

"And it came to pass that Herod, Tetrarch of Judea, did a party throw one night at his palace. And behold! there was much eating and drinking, and noise and merriment, and cracking of coarse jokes and ogling of women and games of footsie under the tables. And all did rejoice, for it was a super banquet and all were determined to have a jolly good time.

And behold! there cometh forth from out of the darkness a voice, which seemeth to come from a subterranean WC or water cistern, for in those times it was kept outdoors. But Herod and the guests heeded the warning not and the feasting did continue. And lo, more wine was passed round and drunk, until everyone present was well-nigh plastered.

And it came to pass that the princess Salome, the beautiful, sexy daughter of Herodias, was present. And overcome by the heat and the noise she did leave the banquet table and did make her way to the terrace, the better to drink in the cool night air thereof, and to escape her stepfather's lustful glances. And behold! as she doth stand there, with her voluptuous figure silhouetted against the shimmering lights of the palace, Naraboth the guard doth murmur "How beautiful is the princess Salome tonight!" for he doth desire her too.

And lo from below there cometh again the voice denouncing Herod for having married his brother's wife. And the princess Salome, turning to Naraboth with a sultry look, did speak thus unto him: "Tell me, thou handsome he-man, whose voice do I hear coming from yonder loo?" 'Tis a strange and sexy voice, and doth turn me on most mightily." But Naraboth is sore afraid and replieth not.

And Salome doth ask Naraboth again about the voice. And lo! captivated by her wondrous beauty Naraboth replieth: "O princess! 'tis the voice of the prophet Jokanaan, whom we call Jok for short but not for long, this being a one-acter. And because thy stepfather Herod doth greatly fear the prophet, he hath him interred in the WC; no one is permitted to see or speak to him, on pain of death".

And it came to pass that the princess Salome, her curiosity aroused by these strange tidings, did bid Naraboth bring the prophet forth. And Naraboth doth obey the royal command and did fetch the prophet from his cell.

And lo, when Jokanaan appeareth from out of the darkness, he did angrily denounce Herod and Herodias and all his court for their corruption and for their gluttony and for their debauchery and their orgies and their perversions and for not inviting him to the party. And lo, when the princess Salome clappeth eyes on this strange man, dressed only in rags and bare skin, a hungry desire for him was born inside her, for she doth find him truly dishy.

And lo! as he doth approach her, she doth desire him more, and as he cometh closer to her she hath the chutzpah to ask to kiss his mouth, saying unto him "Deny me not thy mouth, Jok!" But the prophet heedeth her not, and doth scorn her, and doth call her a daughter of Sodom, and after cursing again Herod and his court, did return to his undergound ablutions.

And it came to pass that Naraboth the guard, fearing greatly the rashness of his act, did take his sword and did kill himself. And behold! the producer was in great distress for he knoweth not how to replace Naraboth in the next act until a stagehand pointeth out that this was a one-acter.

And the night wore on.

And lo! Herod, by now completely sloshed, did leave the banquet table, followed by Herodias and guests, and behold! they did make their way to the terrace, the better to drink the cool night air thereof. And when Herod seeth Salome standing there in all her wondrous beauty his lust for her did akindle anew. And behold! the voice of the prophet is heard again, cursing Herod and warning him not to add incest to injury. But Herod heedeth the warning not and doth continue to gaze lustfully upon his sexy stepdaughter, for he was truly a dirty old man.

And it came to pass that Herod, who enjoyed a bit of erotic after-dinner entertainment, did entreat Salome to dance for him the Dance of the Seven Veils, this being the hottest number in her repertoire. But to tease him Salome doth refuse the Tetrarch's request, saying she knoweth it not. And behold! so great was Herod's desire for this number that he did ask Salome a second time but she doth again refuse, saying she hath brought with her only one veil and for pete's sake how can she perform the Dance of the Seven Veils using only one veil?

And Herod, declining to answer this leading question, doth ask Salome a third time, promising to grant her any wish in return, yea, even half his kingdom. And behold! Salome doth obey her mother's wish and discarding her gown doth don a pair of sexy black fishnets and doth signal the conductor to begin.

And thus it came to pass that the princess Salome did perform the Dance of the Seven Veils before Herod and his court, and that by taking off the veils one by one until none were left did perform the first public performance of striptease in opera, later known as the Gaza Strip, as recorded in Loewenberg's Annals.

And behold! when Salome hath thrown away the last veil, she did reveal herself in all her glory, for she was completely naked. And behold! to cover her nakedness she did throw herself at the feet of Herod who was so delighted by her performance that he doth ask her to name her wish. And now cometh the crunch, for Salome doth ask for the head of Jokanaan.

And behold! Herod doth implore her to choose another gift, but Salome, urged on by Herodias, heedeth him not and doth tell him to stuff it; all she wants is to get ahead. And it came to pass that Herod, seeing that he was out-Heroded, and to cut an overlong one-act opera short, did finally agree to Salome's wish. And behold! that old windbag Herodias did get on the royal hotline to the CEO (Chief Executioner's Officer) and by giving him the Ring of Death did authorise the beheading of the prophet, for it was a Royal Command Performance.

And behold! the CEO did descend into the subterranean WC and lo! a moment later there cometh forth a gasp of horror from the assembled guests, for the head of the prophet doth appear above the cistern upon a silver charger$_{(1)}$. And lo Herod doth exceedingly wroth become and gnasheth his teeth, for his prophet for the year-end trading hath been wiped out.

And it came to pass that when Salome received her share of the prophet, she did gaze upon it with rapture and delight, for it was now hers. And bringing the head of Jokanaan close to her mouth spake thus. "Behold! thy mouth in life thou didst deny me; now it is mine in death!" and she presseth her mouth to his and did his mouth kiss, murmuring ecstatically "Stop thy tickling, Jok".

(1) instead of a severed head a bread loaf may be used, as in Beecham's 1910 production.

And behold! Herod, deeply disgusted by this gruesome spectacle, did turn to his guards and did say unto them: "Porca puttana!" kill that woman!" And the soldiers obeyed and smote her with their shields, and Salome was no more."

# Samson et Dalila

Opera in 3 acts by Camille Saint-Saëns.
First produced Weimar 1877

| | |
|---|---|
| Samson, a Hebrew strongman | tenor |
| Dalila, a Philistine maiden | mezzo |
| High Priest of Dagon (strictly non-kosher) | baritone |
| Abimelech, Claptrap of Gaza | bass |
| An old Hebrew | bass |
| Israelites, Philistines, priests, populance, dancers etc | |
| Scene: Gaza | Time 1150 BC |

*Act 1. A square in Gaza*
And it came to pass that the Children of Israel *were* vanquished by the Philistine hosts and *were* brought before the Temple of Dagon which *doth* stand in the square of Gaza. And behold: they *did* cry out against their cruel captors, for they *were* sorely afflicted and *were* exceedingly browned off.

And behold: a strongman by the name of Samson *did* appear and spake thus unto them: "Hear me, o Children of Israel! I am Samson, son of Sam; I am a strongman, and a *tenore robusto,* and I *will* deliver thee from the Philistine hosts! Await my signal". And lo! the people *did* hear him and *did* cry out "Yea! we have heard thee and *will* hang on and await thy signal". And the people rejoiced.

And lo! there *didst* come into the square their hated foe Abimelech. And behold: when Abimelech saw the Children of Israel in their captivity he *did* cruelly mock them and *did* blaspheme mightily against the God of Israel and *did* sing an exceedingly dull bass aria which no one applauded. And Abimelech was mightily peeved and *did* gnash his teeth and *did* sorely chastise the Children of Israel.

And it came to pass that the spirit of the Lord *did* come upon Samson. And the Lord said unto him "Behold! The time hath come. Rise and go forth and slay the tyrant Abimelech". And Samson rose and went fifth (he was always a late riser) and *did* go into the square. And behold! when he saw Abimelech chastising the Children of Israel he drew forth his jawbone's ass and with a mighty swipe *did* send that uncircumcised dog for six.

And Samson cried out "Here is thy signal, O Israel! Now's yer chance!" And lo! the Children of Israel rejoiced, and *did* throw off their chains of bondage and by throwing rotten eggs at their captors *did* succeed in breaking the Philistine yolk.

And when the High Priest came out of the temple and heard the rumpus in the square, he *did* exceedingly wroth grow. And when he saw the body of Abimelech he *did* a terrible vengeance swear and *did* curse Samson mightily and *did* use language *most* unbefitting a clergyman.

Then from out of the temple came forth many beautiful and *chaste* Philistine maidens led by Dalila, the most beautiful and *chased* of them all. And lo, when she seeth Samson she *did* great homage pay and *did* praise his mighty strength and valour and *did* invite him to come up and see her sometime. And behold! Samson *did* accept her invite for that night for he was smitten by her charms.

And lo! an old Hebrew standing nearby *did* say unto him: "Vot's der *meshuggas?* ain't vun of our girls good enough for you?" But Samson heedeth him not.

*Act 2. Dalila's pad in the Valley of Sorek*
And it came to pass that as Dalila was slipping into something more comfy for her date with Samson there *did* come unto her the High Priest of Dagon. And he said unto her "Behold! when Samson *doth* visit thee tonight, learn of him the secret of his great strength, that we *may* get even with him. If thou wilt do this deed, eleven hundred pieces of silver shalt be thine".  And Dalila *was* mightily pleased at this cash offer, but because the deal was not strictly *kosher,* she *did* insist on payment in advance. And behold: Dalila *did* count it all and found it *was* not wanting except 10% commission for the temple 'poor', ie the High Priest.

And lo: a storm was approaching. And Samson *did* come unto Dalila, for he *was* filled with an insatiable desire for her. And behold, after quenching it with a couple of cokes, Dalila *did* say unto him "Tell me, big boy, what *is* the secret of thy wondrous strength?" But Samson was silent, and replieth not.

And the storm drew closer: and so did Dalila. And behold! she *did* entreat him again and didst offer him wine and all kinds of goodies and did bare her breasts. But our hero was having none of it and replieth not.

And the storm crept closer: and so did Dalila.  And lo: she hath the *chutzpah* to ask Samson a *third* time. And whether it was because of the storm, which was now on top of them, or whether it was because of Dalila, who was now on top of him, Samson could resist no more and *did* reveal unto her the secret of his amazing strength.

"My strength cometh", he said, "from my hair.  If my head be shaven, then my strength *doth* leave me, and I am weak like other men; verily, I say unto thee, it's a case of hair today, gone tomorrow".

And it came to pass that after Dalila *did* sing her hit song Samson *did* give her ample proof of his wondrous strength. And Dalila *was* well pleased, for in one night she had the tables turned, his secret learned, his power spurned, his manhood burned and much silver earned.

And lo, while Samson rested after his performance Dalila *did* cut off his hair, so that he *was* now without his strength and as bald as a badger. And Dalila *was* well pleased, for in one night she had her palm greased, his lust appeased, her prowess teased, his boldness fleeced and his assets seized.

And the Philistines seized him and bound his arms and took him unto Gaza. And Dalila *was* well pleased, for in one night she had his passion dashed, his valour smashed, his machos trashed, her payment cashed and the proceeds stashed.

*Act 3 Scene 1. A prison in Gaza*
And it came to pass that when the Philistines *took* Samson out, they also *took out* his eyes, one by one, and *did* put him in prison. And behold! he was made to turn a great millstone, which even then was considered an awful grind. And the Children of Israel *did* cry out to the Lord, for they *were* again in captivity. But Samson heeded them not, for as Aldous Huxley wrote, he was Eyeless in Gaza.

*Scene 2. The Temple of Dagon*
And it came to pass that the Philistines, in celebration of their victory over Israel, *did* assemble inside the Temple of Dagon. And lo! three thousand more did assemble on the roof. And while the Philistines were busy feasting and drinking there was much dancing and rejoicing, and more wine *was* passed round, and more grub *was* consumed. And lo! Samson was brought into the Temple, and the Philistines *did* mock at his weakness, for what could the poor blighter do now? And Dalila and the High Priest were there and also *did* mock him.

And it came to pass that while these shenanigans *were* at their height Samson *did* turn to the lad who was guiding his steps and said unto him: "Lead me, I pray thee, to the marble pillars that supporteth this temple, that I may rest there awhile, for 'tis jolly tiring standing here". And when the boy had done this Samson said "I beseech thee, o Lord, give me back my strength, just one more time, so that I may get even with these blighters."

And behold, the Lord *did* restore his strength and clasping the two pillars with all his might he *did* emit such a ringing high C that he literally rought down the house, and all inside, including Samson, did perish.

# La sonnambula

Opera in 2 acts by Vincenzo Bellini.
First produced Milan 1831

| | |
|---|---|
| Teresa, owner of a mill | mezzo |
| Amina, her adopted daughter | soprano |
| Elvino, a farmer, bethrothed to Amina | tenor |
| Lisa, owner of the village inn | soprano |
| Count Rodolfo, lord of the manor | bass |

Scene: A Swiss villageTime: early 19th century

*Act 1. Scene 1. The village square*
The villagers are excited about the coming wedding of Amina and Elvino. Amina, an orphan, was adopted by Teresa when still a baby. Lisa the Teaser, as she is known in the village, is also in love with Elvino, or rather his money. Jealous of Amina, she is determined the wedding will not take place.

After Amina has sung her entrance aria Elvino enters, accompanied by a notary. The wedding contract is drawn up and the hungry villagers, alias the chorus, lick their chops at the thought of free grub and booze in the offing. Elvino gives Amina a ring on his mobile and tells her they can now share the same line.

The sound of approaching hooves is heard and a horse and carriage appear. Out steps a handsome stranger, Count Rodolfo, who is returning to his ancestral seat after a long absence, but due to a mix-up in rehearsal schedules Doctor Dulcamara steps out of the carriage instead. He is quickly hustled off stage by the near-apoplectic producer while the horse gives its opinion of the mix-up. After the laughter from the audience has subsided the Count recalls the familiar scenes of his childhood. He then starts to chat up the blushing bride-to-be, much to Elvino's jealousy and Lisa's delight. The latter, combining business with pleasure, invites him to stay the night at her inn, as a paying guest, of course. Lisa's physical charms being no less attractive than Amina's the Count readily accepts.

Teresa now reminds the villagers that the dreaded Phantom of the Opera, said to haunt the village, will soon be putting in its nightly appearance (no marks for recognizing our sleepwalking heroine). As the superstitious villagers wend their way home Elvino and Amina sing a long duet, on the theme of "Anything you can sing I can sing higher", consisting of an ever-elaborating series of trills, runs and *fioriture*, culminating in a high D *in alt*.

*Scene 2. The Count's bedroom at the inn.*
The same evening. The Count, with Lisa in mind, prepares himself a nightcap. There is a quiet knock on the door and on the pretext of "Did you call, sir?" Lisa the Teaser enters. Dressed in a garment as flimsy as her excuse she tells him that the villagers, having discovered his identity, are shortly coming to the inn to welcome him home; in the meantime, she adds, glancing at the bed, she would be pleased to serve *il signor conte*. The Count begins to flirt with her when a noise is heard. Lisa, not wishing to be found in the Count's bedroom, hurries out, but in the rush loses her panties. The Count then conceals himself behind a chair from where he can watch the proceedings.

The Count's bedroom window opens and Amina enters. Unbeknown to the villagers, Amina is a sleepwalker. She wanders about the room in her nightdress, talking to herself about the wedding, as brides tend to do. Then suppressing a yawn she falls asleep on the bed. The Count, realising that Amina is sleepwalking, extinguishes the lights and discreetly withdraws.

It is at this point that Sex raises its Ugly Head. The villagers, having assembled in the inn, make their way to the Count's room to welcome him home. In the dim light they make out the figure of a woman reclining full-length on the Count's bed and withdraw discreetly. But Lisa, having recognised the sleeping beauty, sees her chance. Quickly returning with a lantern she triumphantly shows the villagers, among them Elvino, that the unknown beauty asleep on the count's bed is none other than Amina, their innocent darling of the village.

Scandalised, the villagers raise their voices. Their noise awakens Amina who, understandably, is unable to explain her presence. As Teresa goes over to comfort her, she spies Lisa's panties on the floor and hides them. Elvino and the villagers upbraid Amina for her seeming infidelity and the act closes with our heroine, as *de rigeur* for prima donnas in 19th century opera, obligingly fainting.

*Act 2 Scene 1. A wood outside the village.*
The villagers are on their way to the castle to ask the Count to intervene. Amina meets Elvino who, still believing her to be unfaithful, turns on her angrily. "What were you doing in the Count's bedroom?" he demands fiercely. "I can't possibly conceive", replies the heartbroken heroine. "That's no excuse!" he replies, and snatching the wedding-ring from off her finger, goes off. Poor Amina faints again.

*Scene 2. Outside the mill.*
Meanwhile, Lisa has been busy and has induced Elvino to marry her. Preparations are remade for the reception, much to the delight of the hungry chorus, who sing of the grub and drinks in the offing. The Count enters and tells Elvino he's making a big mistake by marrying Lisa. Amina is innocent: her presence in his bedroom can be explained by the fact that she is a sleepwalker. But Elvino has never heard of sleepwalking, and believes that her visit to the bedroom was for the purpose of *nocturnal copulation* rather than noctambulation.

Teresa appears and on learning that Elvino is to wed Lisa triumphantly produces her panties. She found them, she tells the bewildered Elvino, in the Count's bedroom last night. Lisa arrives and when confronted with the evidence is unable to give an explanation. Elvino feels he's been betrayed a second time: likewise the hungry chorus, who see their prospect of free food and booze disappearing again.

The Count tries once more to convince Elvino of Amina's innocence. "Who can prove it?" Elvino asks. "She herself!" replies the Count, pointing to the mill, and there is Amina, in her nightie, emerging slowly from the mill, sleepwalking again. As she crosses a narrow bridge fording the stream the villagers gasp and hold their breath, for it is known to be unsafe.

As she reaches halfway there is a *crunch!:* a rotten plank gives way and she falls down. For a moment it seems she has fallen into the fast-moving stream below and the assembled villagers gasp and hold their breath a second time but getting to her feet, she continues on her way. She has almost reached the other side of the stream when her billowing nightie catches on a rusty nail and with a sudden tearing sound the nightie comes off completely. For a third time the villagers – and Elvino – gasp, though not for the same reason as before.

At last Amina safely reaches the other side. Teresa covers her with a coat and a joyous shout of *Viva Amina!* goes up from the happy villagers. Elvino, finally convinced of her innocence, replaces the wedding-ring on her finger. Waking from her sleep, Amina sees only the smiling faces of her loved ones. Realising that all is well she bursts into a brilliant *rondo finale* that brings down the house and the opera comes to its happy end.

*Note*
According to secret Covent Garden archives whenever rival sopranos of an Aussie prima donna sang the role of Amina *several* rotten planks mysteriously gave way…

# Tannhäuser

Romantic opera in 3 acts by Richard Wagner.
First produced Dresden 1845

| | |
|---|---|
| Tannhäuser, a late knight | tenor |
| Landgrave of Thuringia | bass |
| Elisabeth, his niece | soprano |
| Wolfram, another late knight | baritone |
| Venus, Goddess of Love | soprano |

Knights, dames, pages, pilgrims etc

Scene: Germany                    Time 13$^{th}$ century

*Act 1. Der Venusberg ('Mount of Venus')*
The curtain rises to reveal Tannhäuser lying exhausted in the arms of Venus, the Goddess of Love, after what has obviously been a fairly steamy session. Awaking from his slumbers, he tells Venus that he's had enough lovemaking for the moment and wants to return to Earth. The goddess, rather like the Marschallin in *Der Rosenkavalier* (an operetta by Strauss) is not getting any younger. Hell having no fury like a woman scorned she curses our hero and predicts that he's gonna be back for more, but being a tenor he takes no notice and leaves.

In the Wartburg valley Tannhäuser meets a procession of pilgrims, among them the Landgrave and Wolfram. They try to persuade him to return and Wolfram tells him his old flame Elisabeth is awaiting him. Sold on the idea of seeing Elisabeth again our hero joins them on their trip back to the Wartburg.

*Act 2. Die Sängehalle ('Hall of Song')*
Having learnt of Tannhäuser's return, Elisabeth is so excited that she sings an aria to an empty hall.
> My lover's coming home at last
> Oh! what a grand occasion!
> My heart is beating twice as fast
> and bursting with elation!

The Landgrave announces a Song Contest, the theme of which is Love with a capital L. The prize, he continues, is the hand of his beautiful niece: the rest of her to follow later. The nobles assemble and the contest begins. First to sing is Wolfram, whose song, in praise of Spiritual Love, is pure and chaste. Next is Tannhäuser. Scornful of Wolfram's noble sentiments he deliberately sings a song in praise of Physical Love, extolling the lusts of the flesh.
>  While lying in the arms of Venus
>  Writing love songs in my sleep
>  The goddess said: "How fine your pen is
>  darling, let me have a peep!"

Not since Wassergate has there been such a *skandal*! The assembled knights, deeply shocked, draw their swords and are about to attack our hero when Liz, with a cry of "*Züruck vom ihm!*" throws herself between them, shielding him from their blades: no mean feat, when she measures three feet across. By pleading for her lover's life she persuades the knights to heed her pleading, which leads to a pleading great ensemble. Tannhäuser's life is spared, on condition that he goes to Rome as a pilgrim and asks the pope's forgiveness for his sin.

*Act 3. Thal vor der Wartburg ('The Wartburg Valley')*
A procession of pilgrims returns from Rome. They are greeted by Liz and Wolfram but Tannhäuser is not among them. Liz goes to pray while Wolfram sings a song to the Evening Star, a popular daily of the time.
>  I like to read the Evening Star
>  it shows who's in the running
>  there's soccer news from near and far
>  its Page Three Girls are stunning!

Eventually our hero stumbles in, looking decidedly grungy. In his Rome Narration he tells Wolfram about his visit to the pontiff.
>  Alas, my meeting with the pope
>  my sin refused to pardon
>  my sole redemption is the hope
>  his staff will sprout and harden
>  Should it bear leaves then I am saved
>  there rests my sole salvation
>  but should it not, my way is paved
>  for Eternal Damnation!

Thoroughly *brauned off* by the pope's harsh judgment our hero calls on the powers of the Goddess of Love. She immediately appears in all her captivating beauty and entices him to return to the pleasures of the Mount of Venus. As Tannhäuser eagerly reaches out to her, Wolfram, still sulking over the song-contest fiasco, shouts out "Hoch Elisabeth!" Venus disappears and in her place rises a pink dawn.

A funeral procession approaches, bearing Elisabeth's body. As Tannhäuser throws himself upon her ice-cold Bier a miracle happens: the pope's staff bursts into leaf! Tannhäuser is redeemed! The pilgrims sing *Hallelujah* and the opera closes.

# *Tosca*

Opera in 3 acts by Giacomo Puccini.
First produced Rome 1900

Characters in order of dying

| | |
|---|---|
| Angelotti, an escaped prisoner | bass |
| Baron Scarpia, chief of police | baritone |
| Mario Cavaradossi, a hack painter | tenor |
| Floria Tosca, a famous diva | soprano |

A sacristan; police agents; soldiers etc

Scene: Rome                                  Time 1800

*Act 1. Interior of the church of Sant'Andrea della Valle*

The opera begins with what Wagnerians call a *Geheimespolizei-kommissarleitmotiv* - three crashing chords depicting the evil, sadistic Baron Scarpia, Chief of Police.

When the curtain rises the stage is empty: Angelotti, the first character to appear, has been caught up in one of Rome's notorious traffic jams while on his way to the church and hasn't arrived yet. A rather rude noise, followed by a voice in desperation exclaiming *"Finalmente!"*, tells us that Angelotti has got rid of what was bothering him. A moment later he enters furtively, still afraid he may have been heard.

It should be explained that Angelotti, ex-leader of the Roman Republic, has just escaped from Castel Sant'Angelo, where he had been imprisoned on the orders of Lady Hamilton, whom he had met by chance in London's Battersea Park Funfair, then the Vauxhall Pleasure Gardens. In his hurry to escape he had forgotten his tuning-fork and now begins a frantic search for the key. Having found it –it was in A flat – he hurriedly takes refuge in a side chapel belonging to the Attavanti family.

A grumpy old busybody of a sacristan enters, shortly followed by Mario Cavaradossi, or Cav for short, a hack painter. Cav has been commissioned to paint the walls of the church and as he wipes his brushes sings the aria *'Reconditioned ammonia'*, a reference to the cleaning agent he uses. A rude noise from the chapel distracts him. Yes, it's Angelotti again who, thinking the coast is clear, has left his hiding place for a quick leak. The two men recognize each other but before they can say *'ciao'* they are interrupted by Tosca's angry voice demanding admittance. Angelotti hurriedly grabs Cav's lunch-basket and hastily retreats to the chapel for a quick nosh-up.

Tosca, a well-stacked prima donna, now makes her dramatic entrance. Dubbed 'The Lay of Ancient Rome' – and not because of her vocal talent either – she walks on in grand style, wearing a low cut long dress, a ridiculous hat and in her hand a staff *alla* Bo-Peep. A jealous woman by nature, she looks around suspiciously and spies a lewd nude sketched by Cav on the church wall. Recognizing the features of a certain marchesa Attavanti – and without her fan, to boot – she flies into a jealous rage and accuses Cav of this, that and the other, more particularly the latter, but after some smooching from the painter she calms down. As he escorts her back to the door he agrees to her parting request to make the blonde nude a brunette – where applicable. At last she leaves.

Cav returns to Angelotti who, having scoffed all the grub, indicates his presence by another rude noise. As the two men hurriedly discuss the political situation a cannon shot is heard: a prisoner has escaped. They leave *subitissimo* for Cav's villa and when Grumpy returns is surprised to find both painter and lunch-basket gone.

Scarpia, accompanied by sinister chords from the pit and by even more sinister henchmen on stage, now makes his appearance. After reprimanding the sacristan for playing with the choirboys in church (*Un tal casino in chiesa*) he examines the evidence and puts together what has happened. His suspicions are confirmed when Tosca returns to tell her lover her plans are changed. By cleverly fanning her jealousy with the Attavanti fan he gets the whole story. As she leaves he orders his men to follow her (aria:*Three beers and a cab*). As the congregation sings a *Te Deum* Scarpia vows to get Angelotti's head, Cav dead and Tosca in bed.

*Act 2. The Palazzo Farnese*
The night of 14 June, and a few hours later. To celebrate the defeat of Napoleon a grand reception is to be held in the palazzo, with lots of free booze and grub and a concert by Tosca. In his apartments the police chief pours himself a *Farnese Fizz* and muses over his plans. Having laid a trap for the painter, he tells himself, the next person to be laid is la diva.

A sudden knock on the door interrupts his erotic thoughts. Spoletta, a police agent, reports that he followed Tosca to Cav's villa without finding Angelotti; he has arrested the painter instead. "Bring him in!" orders the police chief, returning to his drink and the erotica pages of *Il Cafone*. Cav is led in, paintbrush in hand. Scarpia, who fancies himself as a TV quizmaster, begins by asking where Angelotti is hiding but when Cav refuses to answer he turns nasty.

"Think carefully, cavaliere", he warns, addressing the painter by his title, "we have ways of making you talk; we have even been known to make tenors sing in tune!" Tosca arrives and the cross-examination resumes but when Cav continues to play dumb Scarpia loses his temper and orders him to be taken to the torture-chamber for 'questioning', as it is euphemistically called in certain countries.

This particular task is performed by Roberti, or Bob for short, a sort of odd-jobs man. His speciality is extracting information from reluctant prisoners by extracting their teeth (without an anaesthetic) or by pulling their legs (without a joke). An ex-bongo player, he begins his performance with the so-called "Steel Band" act, a spiked steel hoop attached to Cav's temples which is tightened each time he refuses to answer.

"Increase the torture!" orders the sadistic Scarpia when Cav refuses to talk and Bob obligingly obliges. Finally, as her tortured lover's screams become unbearable Tosca breaks down and reveals where Angelotti is hiding."Well, well, well", is Scarpia's cynical comment. Cav is brought in and Scarpia sends his men to arrest Angelotti.

Just then an agent bursts in with the news that Napoleon, instead of being defeated, has been victorious. Our hero, a staunch Republican, gets to his feet, and despite his gruelling torture sings "Vittoria, vittoria" on a succession of high A flats. It is his death-warrant. Scarpia, a fanatical Royalist, orders his immediate execution and Cav is led off between guards. Tosca and Scarpia are left alone in his apartment.

"How about a drink?" Scarpia suggests. "How much?" asks Tosca suspiciously. "It's on the house", he replies gallantly. "Not the drink, you idiot!" retorts the exasperated diva, "what's your price for freeing Cav?" His reply is to make a grab for her.

It is at this highly dramatic moment that Puccini introduces some much-needed comic relief. Accordingly we witness the hilarious spectacle of a lecherous middle-aged police chief chasing a well-endowed prima donna round the stage in a vain attempt to extract from her the 'price' which he wants but she doesn't want to pay.

The comic episode over, the exhausted diva collapses onto a sofa. Secretly, she has enjoyed being chaste, but enough is enough. Suddenly, drums are heard: her lover, explains Scarpia, is being escorted to the scaffold. Our heroine falls to the floor where, at a sign from the prompter, she sings her celebrated aria *Lovin' music*.

After the applause has subsided an agent enters with the news that Angelotti, having betrayed his hiding-place by another rude noise, had taken an overdose of aspirins and now lies dead; the other prisoner is awaiting his fate. Scarpia turns to Tosca for her answer: is the 'price' acceptable? Sorrowfully she nods her consent, then buries her face in the cushions.

The police chief now gives careful instructions to his agent. To simulate Cav's death, a mock execution is to be carried out, after which Cav's body is to be carried out. The agent departs and Scarpia now turns to what may be described as more pleasant business. Pouring himself a 'Palmieri Special', and with a smile as false as his teeth, he approaches Tosca to claim his 'reward'.

An old hand at the game, the diva has no intention of letting him have it right away. First, she demands that all precautions be taken. Scarpia accordingly goes to his desk, produces a safe-conduct (as it was called in those days) and returning to Tosca stretches out his arms to receive her kiss. Instead of a kiss she produces a fruit-knife taken earlier from the table and stabs him through the heart. He falls dead at her feet. Bending over the body, Tosca deftly removes the safe-conduct from the dead man's hand, then placing two Roman candles on either side, she lights the blue touch-paper and steals silently away.

As she reaches the door, she takes a long, backward glance at the prostrate body of Rome's late chief of police. Then turning to the audience, she utters the immortal phrase "Era lui che fregava tutta Roma!" and tiptoes away into the night.

*Act 3. The battlements of Castel Sant'Angelo*

Some hours later. In the background can be seen the dome of St Peters silhouetted against the night sky, while nearby the lights of Vatican City and other famed Roman nightspots twinkle enticingly. The song of a shepherd (*É la solita storia del pastore*) is heard in the distance as he calls his flock.

Dawn is breaking and the orchestra plays a shortened version of the tenor's big aria to make sure he remembers it later. Cav is then led in and a gaoler cheerfully tells him that he has one hour to live. Offering the gaoler a ring (aria: *Prendi l'anel ti dono*) Cav asks for pen and ink: he forgot to fill in his last football coupon and Juventus is playing Lazio. He then sings his big aria about the stars shining etc.

Tosca, who has been waiting in the wings, hurries onstage and breathlessly tells Cav what has happened. *"Merde!"* he ejaculates; "No, *murder*" she replies, correctly his abominable French accent. She then instructs him how to act before the firing-squad: when the soldiers open fire he must fall down as dead. "Easy" says Cav (he'll never know how easy). He must then wait until she gives the signal for him to get up. Cav says OK and awaits the firing-squad.

The soldiers march in, line up and fire. *"Ecco un artista!"* exclaims Tosca admiringly as her lover falls convincingly to the ground. The soldiers leave and she whispers to him not to move yet, an instruction he carefully obeys. The last soldier leaves and Tosca urges Cav to get up. When he doesn't she realizes the awesome truth: Not only did Scarpia *fregava tutta Roma*, but *aveva fregato anche lei:* real bullets were used and her lover lies dead.

Scarpia's men can now be heard angrily mounting the stairs: his body has been discovered. Running to the lift, our heroine tries to outwit her pursuers by going down as they are coming up, but lacking the 50 cent coin needed to operate it she dashes instead to the parapet to prepare for flight – literally, as events turn out. As the men close in, Tosca leaps onto the parapet. Half turning towards them, and with the final cry of *"Scarpia! avanti a Dio!* she hurls herself over the edge.

# La Traviata

Opera in 3 acts.by Giuseppe Verdi.
First produced Venice 1853

| | |
|---|---|
| Violetta Valéry, a courtesan<br>'Vi' to her friends | prima donna assoluta |
| also ran:<br>Alfredo Germont, known as 'Alf' | tenor |
| Giorgio Germont, his father | baritone |
| Annina, Violetta's maid | soprano |
| Flora Bervoix, a friend of Violetta's<br>and in the same line of business | mezzo |
| Gaston, Alf's friend | tenor |
| Baron Douphol, Violetta's admirer | baritone |
| Doctor Grenvil, a quack | bass |

Servants, guests, dancers etc

Scene: Paris and environs            Time; 1850

*Act 1. Vi's salon in Paris.*
The opera begins with a celebrated prelude, in which the musically-educated will immediately recognize the hit song of the 1930s, *Hear my song, Violetta.*

The curtain goes up to reveal a swinging party. Vi is giving an 'at home', the bubbly's flowing like champers and there's lots of good grub in the offing. Among the guests is Gaston, who introduces Vi to his friend Alf. It seems that Alf prefers to be known socially as Germont *fils*. With a name like Alf, who can blame him?

Vi proposes a toast, Melba style, and turning to Baron Douphol, her present admirer, asks him to sing a drinking song. The baron refuses and sulks: this is because Verdi made him a baritone instead of a tenor and he can't reach the high notes. Vi then turns to Alf who being a tenor, readily accepts. So begins the brindisi, led by Alf and Vi and joined by the hungry chorus who this way hope to get in on the free food and drink on offer.

Vi is about to lead the company into another room for dinner and dancing when she suddenly feels faint. It should be mentioned that Vi is dying of consumption, a fact not always apparent in performance. Sitting down, she tells the hungry chorus to go in without her, which they do with relish. As she looks at herself in the mirror she sees how pale she is. She then catches sight of Alf's reflection.

This is Alf's big chance. Pouring out his love, his soul and a vermouth he asks Vi to come and live with him in the country, the arrangement being that she pays the rent and expenses. Vi laughs at the idea but after he and the guests leave she considers the offer. Is this Mr Right, she asks herself as she begins her famous *scena:* with a name like Alf, how can she be sure? Dismissing the idea as folly she launches into a brilliant cabaletta that brings down the curtain while her E flat *in alt.* brings down the house.

*Act 2 Scene 1. A country house near Paris.*
Interior of a drawing room. Alf enters from the garden carrying a shotgun, which he uses to keep away creditors. He tells us that he and Vi have been living together for some three moons and that they're still over the moon. Annina, Vi's maid, hurries in. On learning that Vi has been selling off her jewellery to pay for his singing lessons Alf is filled with remorse. Bidding Annina to say nothing to her mistress, ie *his* mistress, he dashes off to Paris in search of Louis.

Vi enters, reading an invitation from Flora to a party in Paris that evening. A visitor is announced who introduces himself as Germont *père.* He informs Vi that she must break off *toute suite* her liaison with Germont *fils* because it is causing *un scandale terrible* and is threatening the wedding of his young *fille, mais oui.* Vi protests that she truly loves *fils* and cannot live without him but *père* won't budge. Vi tearfully fully agrees to his request and sitting at a table begins writing a 'Dear John'. Germont *père,* unaccustomed to so much excitement in one day, goes into the garden and takes up a position behind a tree.

Alf suddenly appears. Ignoring his questions Vi takes a heartbreaking farewell and accompanied by Annina dashes off to Paris. A servant enters and hands Alf Vi's letter. Just then his father comes in *pp* from the garden. Having read the letter Alf vows revenge, and seeing Flora's invite on the table dashes off to Paris. Germont *père,* finding himself alone in a deserted house in the country with nothing to do, reckons he may as well join Flora's party and dashes off to Paris just as the curtain falls.

*Scene 2. Flora's salon in Paris*
Another swinging party. Guests dressed up as gypsies, matadors and picadors dance and frolic about. Alf arrives and immediately makes for the gaming tables. Soon after Vi enters, escorted by old Douphol, to whom she has given her arm: her heart, we understand, still belongs to Alf.

Meanwhile, Alf has been having fantastic luck at the tables and as he rakes in his winnings makes insulting remarks about Vi. Douphol challenges him at cards but Alf's luck continues to hold. The announcement that supper is being served gives the baron a welcome excuse to leave.

Vi and Alf are left alone. After a bitter exchange of words Vi falsely admits she loves the baron. The enraged Alf calls in the chorus from the supper room – they're needed anyway for the act 2 finale – and with a display of bad manners exceeding that of a popstar publicly "pays off" Vi with his winnings. As befitting a prima donna assoluta Vi promptly faints but recovers later to sing *Alfredo, Alfredo*. Who then turns up but Germont *père*. In a trembling voice he denounces his son as unworthy of his name. Alf, ashamed of having publicly insulted a lady, hangs his head and the act closes with a mighty anti-Alf ensemble (1)

*Act 3. Vi's bedroom.*
Vi is mortally ill. Doc Grenvil enters and assures Vi she's getting better but on leaving whispers to Annina that her mistress has but a few hours to live. Some doctor... In a letter from Germont *père* Vi reads that the baron has been wounded in a duel and that Alf has fled abroad to avoid the police but on learning of Vi's sacrifice is on his way back. Annina rushes in with the news that Alf has returned and a moment later the two lovers are together. But it's too late and Vi falls exhausted into chair. Taking a snapshot from out of her drawers she gives it to Alf and with her dying breath reminds him not to forget to water the camellias.

---

(1) Germont père, that staunch guardian of bourgeois morality, clearly knows his way around the maisons de Paris; within a few hours of leaving a demi-mondaine's country-house outside Paris he's inside the Paris house of another one.

# *Tristan und Isolde*

*Opera in 3 acts by Richard Wagner. First produced Munich 1865*

| | |
|---|---|
| Tristan, a Corny knight | tenor |
| Isolde, an Irish princess | soprano |
| Mark, king of Cornwall | bass |
| Brannigan, Isolde's Irish maid | soprano |
| Kurwenal, retainer to Tristan | baritone |
| Melot, a courtier | tenor |

Scene: Cornwall and Brittany          Time: Legendary

Introduction
Isolde, an extremely beautiful but highly neurotic Irish princess, is on her way to England, there to become the bride of King Mark. The old king, who should have known better, has entrusted her to the care of his favourite knight Tristan, who is also his nephew. However, human nature being what it is, the inevitable occurs.

*Act 1. On board the Belfast-Cornwall ferryboat.*
The beautiful princess Isolde is lying prostrate on a couch, bemoaning her sad fate. It has been a rough crossing and the princess, who is travelling steerage (King Mark is too mean to pay $2^{nd}$ class) has been violently seasick. This, coupled with her intense hatred of the knight Tristan - actually a peculiar form of love-hate not uncommon between sopranos and tenors in opera – has roused her fiery Irish temper to boiling point. This explains why everyone else on board has taken refuge behind a curtain for safety.

After a spell at running down Tristan, King Mark and Marriage in general our temperamental princess calls out to Brannigan and asks her where they are. "Just rounding the Lizard, maam" bawls back the maid from behind the curtain, returning to the arms of the first mate who has been demonstrating a sailor's knowledge of matters navel. A sudden lurch of the ship causes our princess to utter another right royal curse. "Better death" she cries, "than to stay on this accurséd ship!" and she commands the maid to bring Tristan to her immediately. But when Brannigan tries to approach the knight his servant Kurwenal intervenes and rudely informs the maid to tell her mistress to get laid. By a curious coincidence this is actually what happens in act 2.

Brannigan informs Isolde of Kurwenal's answer and her mistress's temper knows no bounds. "Roight!" declares the princess in a thick Irish brogue, " Oi'll teach that insolent knight a lesson" and taking a phial of poison from a golden casket left over from the previous night's performance of *Faust* she orders Brannigan to pour the contents into a goblet. Like Carmen in the Card Scene, Isolde is determined that death will be their united destiny.

And so it would have been had not that dumb maid committed one of the classic boo-boos in all opera. You remember the scene in *Trovatore* where Azucena mixes up the two babies? Brannigan, having left her specs on deck, mixes up the two phials. Instead of pouring out the death-potion, that *Dummkopf* of a skivvy pours out a love-potion, altering the entire course of Anglo-Irish history and Wagnerian music-drama as well.

As the ship nears port Tristan enters and Isolde, with a meaningful glance, offers him the fatal goblet. Our hero takes a good long swig and hands the goblet back to Isolde, who drains it to the last drop. Death at long last, she exclaims joyfully. But this being opera the opposite happens: instead of dropping dead on the spot, both of them are overcome by such a driving sexual urge that they fall into each other's arms and narrowly miss flying overboard in their ecstasy. The ship reaches shore but the couple are in such a dazed state that they don't know whether they're coming or going. The curtain descends and we have to wait until act 2 to discover the full consequences of Brannigan's blundering bloomer.

*Act 2. Cornwall by night.*
The second act of this mighty, immortal love story takes place in Cornwall. Isolde, now queen, is still under the influence of the love-potion and can think of nothing else except Tristan. King Mark and his followers have gone off hunting and are not expected back until late, leaving the way clear for The Big Meeting.

When the curtain rises Brannigan is in the garden, listening intently for the king's horn while Isolde impatiently awaits the arrival of Tristan. The maid, aware of the consequences of such indiscretion, begs her to take care but Isolde laughs and dismisses her fears as 'blarney'. Seizing a flaming torch she hurls it to the ground. She then takes a scarf and waving it to and fro six times signals for her lover to appear. According to Freud, the waving of the scarf six times represents a kind of mystical *sechs symbol.*

Our hero, waiting in the wings, rushes onstage. According to the stage directions at this point the two lovers rush into each other's arms in a passionate embrace. Unfortunately, due to the surrounding darkness – Wagner *would* insist on a total blackout – they miss each other and start groping around in the dark. *"Isolde! Isolde!"* the knight calls out . *"Tristan!*

*Tristan!"* yells back the distraught queen. Eventually, with the assistance of the stage electrician and a torch, the two lovers are finally united and the action is resumed, much to the delight of the audience.

We now reach the climax of this passionate love scene (the two lovers reach theirs later). Tristan draws his beloved down onto what the libretto describes as a 'flowery bank' where, to Wagner's sublime love music, they proceed to make love sublimely. So begins what is generally regarded as the greatest love duet in opera; being by Wagner it is also the longest. By the time it's finished dawn has broken and the two lovers are utterly exhausted: likewise the audience.

It is in this rather compromising situation that the lovers are discovered. Brannigan, acting as look-out, lets out a cry of warning while Kurwenal, sword in hand and heart in mouth, rushes in shouting *"Save thyself, Tristan!"* But it is too late: our hero, having spent everything he had, is unable to save even a penny. A moment later hubby enters, accompanied by Melot and other knights.

Given the circumstances, it must be said that the king takes his wife's adultery with his nephew very philosophically. After ticking off Tristan he asks for an explanation, but as none is forthcoming nothing further is said. Tristan turns to Isolde and asks if she will follow him to the land of his birth: after such a steamy session, Isolde declares ecstatically, she'll follow him anywhere. By way of reply Tristan kisses her gently.

This seeming act of further treachery proves too much for the zealous Melot who, drawing his sword, challenges Tristan to a duel. Our hero, always the gentleman, refuses to raise his sword against a friend (the fact that he is *unable* to raise it following his love making marathon is discreetly ignored by the producer) and receives the full thrust of Melot's blade. Mortally wounded, Tristan falls to the ground and the curtain does likewise.

*Act 3. Tristan's castle in Brittany.*
The last act of this mighty, immoral love story takes place in Brittany, to where the faithful Kurwenal has brought his dying master. We learn that Tristan has been lying unconscious in the courtyard of his castle since arrival, Kurwenal having forgotten to bring the keys. We further learn that Tristan's wound, unlike Amfortas', can only be healed by a woman. Kurwenal has sent Isolde an SMS and her arrival is expected as soon as the British Rail ferry strike is settled.

To help pass the time a shepherd, left over from the last act of *Tosca,* has been engaged by the management to play a tune on his pipe. Although Wagner composed a song for the shepherd to play in this act he prefers to play such favourites as *Frère Jacques, Au clair de la lune* or *Alouette*. These have the advantage of adding local colour to an otherwise static act and keeping the audience guessing as to what tune the shepherd's going to play next.

As Tristan listens he relives his moments of passion with the passionate Irish queen. Suddenly there is a change in the shepherd's song: Isolde's ship is sighted! As the faithful Kurwenal hurries to the shore to help her disembark our hero, in the mistaken belief that another steamy session is due, feverishly tears off his bandages. A moment later Isolde appears and with a great cry of "*Tristan!*" throws herself at full force into his arms. But alas! it is too much for our weakened hero. No longer able to sustain the force of 120kg of solid soprano flesh hurtling through the air he collapses under the onslaught and with a final groan falls to the ground.

In the meantime a second ship carrying King Mark, Melot and others has cast anchor. Brannigan having told the king about switching the potions Mark has come to pardon his erring knight-errant but it is too late: Tristan is dead. The faithful Kurwenal, enraged by the death of his master, challenges Melot to a duel and slays him on the spot, but in so doing receives his own death wound.

It now only remains for Isolde to make up the fatal foursome. Like Brünnhilde, she feels she has nothing left to live for; besides, it's past midnight and it's about time this overlong opera came to an end. At a cue from the conductor she begins her *Liebestod* and on the words *Unbewusst, hochste Lust!* falls dying on her late lover's prostrate form.

And so, five hours and four bodies later, the curtain falls on this sagacious saga of salacious sexuality. Although the libretto gives no explanation about Isolde's death – before the *Liebestod* she appeared to be in excellent health – rumour hath it that Brannigan, in order to atone for her earlier clanger, remembered her specs and this time gave her mistress the right potion.

# *Il trovatore*

Opera in 4 axe, the last reserved for the tenor.
Music by Giuseppe Verdi.
First produced Rome 1853

| | |
|---|---|
| Leonora, lady-in-waiting to the queen | soprano |
| Ines, her confidante | mezzo |
| Manrico, a troubadour and supposed son of | tenor |
| Azucena, a gypsy woman | mezzo |
| Count di Luna, a Spanish nobleman | baritone |
| Ferrando, captain of the guard | bass |
| A messenger; soldiers, gypsies, etc | |

Scene: Spain                              Time: $15^{th}$ century

*Il Trovatore is the story of The Eternal Triangle, with a baby thrown in — literally — for good measure…*

*Act 1. Scene 1. A hall in the Count's palace*
Midnight is approaching. The Count's soldiers are on guard duty, ie snoozing, smoking and loafing. Bored with nothing to do they ask Ferrando, their captain, to tell them, for the umpteenth time, the story of the Count's missing brother.

"It was a dark and stormy night", begins Ferrando, lighting up a quick fag, "when, about 25 years ago, during the Great Fuel Crisis, an old gypsy woman was found inside the palace rooms leaning over the cradle of the younger brother, then a baby. On the orders of the Count's father she was arrested and burnt alive at the stake. To avenge her mother's death the daughter stole into the castle, stole the baby and flung him into a fire" (shouts of *qual'orrore!* from the chorus). "Despite every effort", continues Ferrando, "the gypsy woman was never found. The Count's father, however, believing the boy was still alive, charged his son to continue the search for his missing brother".

What Ferrando *doesn't* know is that Azucena, having lost her specs in the kerfuffle, had thrown her *own* baby into the flames by mistake, and has brought up the stolen baby as her own (aria: *O mio bambino caro*). And what Azucena *doesn't* know is that, as a result of her boo-boo, the baby was later destined to become the tenor to sing *Di quella pira* with its top C. Is the truth discovered about the wrong baby?   For the answer to this burning question, read on...

*Scene 2. The palace gardens*

The same night and very dark. The beauteous Leonora, the queen's lady-in-waiting, is herself laying in waiting for the appearance of a troubadour with whom she has fallen head over spurs in love. She tells Ines that he comes to serenade her knightly, accompanied by his loot.  By a strange coincidence Count di Luna, also in love with Leonora, has chosen this same night to court her.

Suddenly, the voice of the troubadour is heard offstage singing his party piece (*A wand'ring minstrel I*). The Count steps forward and to his delight is passionately embraced in the darkness by Leonora. The maddened troubadour removes his helmet (how he sang with it on is known only to the producer) and furiously upbraids Leonora for her seeming unfaithfulness.  It is only when the moon re-appears from behind a cloud that Leonora realises she has embraced the wrong lover. Blaming the darkness for her blunder (aria: *Nel buio non si vede un pazzo*) our heroine manages to placate the sulking tenor. Her soothing words, however, only inflame the jealous Count who draws his sword and the two men fight it out. Leonora, as befitting a Verdian heroine, does the only decent thing and faints and we have to wait until the next act to find out who beat who.

*Act 2 Scene 1. A gypsy encampment* [1]

Azucena recounts to the troubadour, *aka* Manrico her son, the events leading to her mother's horrible death and begs him to avenge her. Manrico tells her that in a recent fight with the Count, he had his rival at his mercy but a voice from heaven bade him spare the Count's life.  "*Strana pietà!*" *(You bloody fool!)* is his mother's cryptic comment.

---

[1] Producers on shoestring budgets can use the same set as for act 3 of Carmen; thanks to the overall darkness no one will notice the difference.

Suddenly a messenger, obviously new to the part, rushes in and breathlessly announces that the gypsy has been captured by the Count's men and is about to be burnt at the stake. In desperation the prompter frantically signals to the messenger that this line belongs to the *next* act. Red-faced, the messenger exits hastily and returns immediately, this time with the correct announcement that Leonora, believing her lover to be dead, is about to enter a convent. Manrico dashes off to rescue her.

*Scene 2. The cloisters of a convent.*

Led by a chorus of nuns, Leonora and Ines sorrowfully enter, Leonora grieving at the loss of Manrico, Ines at the loss of her job. As Leonora bids farewell to life the Count and his men spring out from behind some bushes: Manrico and his men do likewise and a fierce vocal battle, in the best Verdian style, develops. The curtain comes down on a noisy ensemble, with Manrico the winner, the Count the loser and Leonora in ecstasy at being saved from the cloisters.

*Act 3. Scene 1. The Count's encampment.*
Di Luna's soldiers sing a song in praise of war. Azucena, found wandering around the camp peddling contraband cigarettes, has been arrested as a suspicious character. By one of those rare coincidences in Italian opera she is recognised by Ferrando as the same gypsy woman who stole the Count's brother all those years ago. In desperation she calls out to her son for help. The Count orders his men to light a fire, for Azucena, like her mother before her, is to be burnt at the stake (medium rare). As the flames begin to rise, things start hotting up for the Count and even more for the gypsy.

*Scene 2. Manrico's fortress of Castellor.*
Back at the ranch things are also hotting up. Manrico and Leonora are about to tie the knot, and as the loving couple walk towards the chapel to the strains of nuptial music, an organ begins to swell. But their dream is shattered when a messenger enters with the news that the Count is keeping mum: the pyre has already been lit, he tells the frustrated bride-to-be, and if Manrico doesn't get a move on mum will soon become *arrosto alla zingara*. Hurriedly collecting his sword, his men and his wits, Manrico launches into *Di quella pira,* the *stretta* famous for the top C *not* written by Verdi, and dashes off again to the rescue.

*Act 4 Scene 1. Exterior of the Count's palace.*
Manrico's rescue bid, as the tabloids like to call it, has failed, and on the Count's orders he and Azucena have been thrown into prison to await execution. Leonora slowly enters; on her finger is a ring containing a swift poison. The *Miserere* begins, chanted offstage by monks in their dirty habits: that's why they're not seen on stage. Manrico, imprisoned inside the tower, answers Leonora's anguished cries from outside the tower: how they can possibly hear each other is known only to the stage manager.

The *Miserere* over, the soprano steps forward to receive her plaudits only to find that the tenor has bribed the gaoler with a packet of fags and now appears on stage to share her applause. Hiding her fury behind a false smile she bows gratefully to the audience but gets her revenge in the next scene by secretly substituting a real axe for the stage prop.

As Leonora exits the Count enters and gives orders for the execution of his rival and the burning of the gypsy. But where is Leonora, the Count asks? By a strange coincidence rare in Italian opera Leonora overhears this question and throwing herself at the Count's feet pleads for her lover's life: *"My reward?"* asks the Count? *"Me!"* she replies. The Count, flushed with triumph, agrees and gives orders for the troubadour's release. As he does so Leonora secretly takes a quick nip of poison from the ring on her finger. *"M'avrà"* she mutters, *"ma fredda!"* Well, some like it hot.

*Scene 2. A prison cell*
After our eyes have become accustomed to the darkness (each act in this opera gets progressively darker - increasing the atmosphere of gloom-and-doom) we make out the reclining figures of Manrico and Azucena.

Mother and son sing a mournful duet recalling happier times and the old gypsy falls asleep. Leonora hurries in, having bribed the gaoler with more fags. Breathlessly, for she hasn't got much left, she tells the prisoner that he is free but suspecting the price she has paid, he curses her for not getting him 10%.

By this time Leonora's poison has done its work. Suddenly feeling faint she confesses and with a final cry falls dead into Manrico's arms. The Count, realising he's been double-crossed, orders the immediate execution of the prisoner. As Manrico is led away, Azucena awakes. The Count leads her to the window, from where she is just in time to see her son get it in the neck. As he loses his head, Azucena loses hers, and in an exultant voice tells the Count he has just murdered his own brother. *"Sei vendicata, o madre!"* she cries on a high B flat, which evidently proves too much for her, for she too dies, leaving the grief-stricken Count with three corpses, a blood-stained axe and another lit pyre to extinguish.

> *Envoi*
> So ends the story of *Il trovatore*
> a terrible tale of lust
> with singers illogical and fees astronomical
> no wonder that Opera's gone bust!

# *Turandot*

Opera in 3 acts by Giacomo Puccini.
First produced Milan 1926

| | |
|---|---|
| Turandot, an icy princess | soprano |
| Calaf, a hot prince | tenor |
| Loo, a slavegirl | soprano |
| Altoum, Emperor and Turandot's dad | tenor |
| Timur, Calaf's dad | bass |
| Ping, Pang, Pong | 2 tenors 1 baritone |
| Guards, courtiers, executioner, populance etc | |
| Scene: China | Time: legendary |

*Act 1. Square One.*
As the sun sets in Peking, a vast crowd of Pekinese gathers in the square to hear the results of the contest between Princess Turandot and her latest contender, the Prince of Persia. A mandarin appears and unrolling a scroll, reads out a royal decree over the tannoy: "Turandot the Chased will become the bride of a prince of royal blood if he can solve three riddles; if he fails he shall lose his head ('testa'); hence the so-called 'Testa Match'.

Having failed, the Prince of Persia is to be executed tonight, when the moon has risen (chorus: The moon hath raised her gamp). The Pekinese in the square, straining at their leashes, surge forward demanding blood, the recent drought having made them thirsty. Among them is Calaf, the Unknown Prince. Hearing a cry for help, he finds an old man who's been knocked down by the surging mob. It is his long-lost father Timur, King of Tartar Sauce, who was forced to flee his country, accompanied only by Loo, a little slavegirl. Although father and son rejoice at being reunited Calaf begs Timur not to address him by name as this could give the game away in act 3, causing him to lose his head.

As the sky grows darker and the moon brighter the crowd's excitement mounts and the people cry out for the Executioner to start work. A funeral procession, led by priests, mandarins and clementines, crosses the stage; the last figure is the Prince of Persia, sad and dignified (aria: I've got those Chinese laundry blues). Behind him walks the giant Executioner waving his enormous chopper (Confucius he say: if you want to get ahead, get a chopper).

The crowd, moved by the Prince's plight, begs the Princess to spare his life; Calaf calls out to her to appear on the balcony. At a sign from the prompter she does so and Calaf is dazzled by her blinding beauty. Coldly giving the 'thumbs down' sign, the Princess returns to her interrupted dinner of chop suey and noodles. A world-famous diva, she feels she's already done enough in this act for free. A clause in her contract stipulates she is to appear only in acts 2 and 3 so why bother with act 1I? - she doesn't get paid for it.

The moment of reckoning for the Prince has arrived. His head is placed on the block, the Executioner's chopper comes down and zap: That Was The Peke That Was. The Prince's head, after being shown to the populance, is carefully packed away by the Props Manager: princes' heads, like those of prophets[1] being hard to come by since the Recession. Calaf, bewitched by the Princess' fatal beauty, strides to the gong and is just about to strike it when he is blocked in mid-aria by two courtiers barring his way. They are Ping and Pong, a Chinese table-tennis team introduced by the librettists to add a touch of comedy to an otherwise grisly scene. Pang, a third team member who acts as relief player – hence Pee for relief – arrived too late for rehearsals and was unable to play in act 1.

Ping-Pong try to dissuade Calaf from entering the contest by telling him it's been rigged by the trade unions to prevent the Executioner from being made redundant. Timur and Loo then add their pleas but Calaf ignores them. Seizing the hammer of the gong he strikes it three times: going, going, gong. The sound reverberates throughout the city, announcing that another foolish contender is about to lose his head.

*Act 2. Scene 1. A pavilion in the Imperial Gardens.*
Ping, Pong and Pang are bemoaning the fate of their beloved China. Ping sings of his home in the country, Pong about his distant forest and Pang about his garden at Kiu (change at Earls Court for Richmond Line). A flourish of strumpets interrupts them and they make their way to the palace to attend the contest.

---

(1) see Salome

*Scene 2. The palace square.*
A mighty throng fills the square. At the top of an immense staircase stand eight Wise Guys with sealed scrolls containing the answers to the three riddles. Toughies from the CIA (Chinese Imperial Army – not to be confused with the Central Intelligence Agency) keep a close eye on the scrolls to ensure the answers are not leaked to the press. In a nearby betting shop, cleverly disguised as a pagoda, bookmakers offer odds of 500 to 1 against the Unknown Prince, totally unaware that his victory is shortly going to make them bankrupt.

Old Emperor Altoum, seated on a throne as ancient as himself, declares the contest open. A group of virgins enter and strew flowers on the staircase for Turandot's entrance. A moment later the Princess makes her long-awaited appearance. Taking her cue from a song in *Kiss me, Kate*, she explains why she hates men so much. A thousand thousand years ago, she says, there lived happily in this palace a beautiful princess named Ting-a-ling, but when the barbarian hordes invaded China she was abducted, tortured and slain – "by a man just like you " she tells Calaf. In revenge she has vowed that no man shall ever possess her. Having explained her credo, she now turns to our hero and poses Riddle No1.

"What is it", she asks Calaf, "that a man stands up to do, a woman sits down to do, and a dog holds out his leg to do?". After a pause, Calaf replies "To shake hands, o mighty Princess!" There is a stunned moment of silence as the eight Wise Guys consult their scrolls: the Stranger's answer is correct! As loud cheers go up from the crowd the bookmakers' odds go down to 100 to 1.

Angered by the Stranger's prompt reply, the haughty princess descends a few steps and, facing our hero, poses Riddle no2. "Why is rape impossible?" she asks. Calaf, suddenly remembering the words of the wise Confucius, boldly replies "Rape is impossible, o princess, because Woman with skirt up runs faster than Man with trousers down!". The eight Wise Guys consult their scrolls. Yes! the Stranger's answer is correct. The people shout for joy but the princess, like another royal personage, is not amused and orders her guards to whip them into silence. In the meantime the bookmakers' odds have slipped to 20 to 1.

Having lost her cool, the once-proud princess now descends to the foot of the staircase and looking Calaf straight in the eye – or as best her squint will allow – furiously hurls at him Riddle No3. "Where is it", she growls menacingly, " that a girl's hair grows thickest and blackest and curliest?"

Our hero is at a loss: try as he may he's stumped for an answer. Puccini's skill as an orchestrator is here revealed: to portray the intricate workings of the tenor's brain the orchestra at this point remains muta. The princess, assured of her victory, declares that Calaf has failed, but with a sudden flash of inspiration he jumps to his feet : "I have the answer: in Central Africa!"

For the third time the eight Wise Guys look to their scrolls and for the third time the answer is correct: the Stranger has solved all three riddles! The populance, delirious with joy, bursts into shouts of jubilation. As for old Altoum, he is so chuffed at having got his unmarried daughter off his hands that he dances a wild jig up and down the staircase. The bookmakers, facing financial ruin, make a dash for the exits but are arrested by the CIA. The only other person, apart from the irate princess, who refuses to join in the celebrations is the Chief Executioner. Having been made redundant, he packs up his belongings and quietly slips out by a back door.

But Turandot refuses to accept defeat. She may be icy and cold but she knows how to turn the heat on. In what the tabloids like to call a surprise turnabout she declares she will be possessed by no man, whether he be prince or pauper, tenor or bass. The emperor reminds her that the oath is sacred but she tells him defiantly "non mi frega per niente!". At this dramatic retraction of the marriage vows Calaf makes Turandot an offer she cannot refuse: if she can discover his name before dawn he is prepared to die; if she fails, she will be his bride. Turandot nods her acceptance and the curtain falls.

*Act 3.*
*Scene 1. The palace gardens.*
It is night, as evidenced by the darkness on stage. Voices of heralds are heard. By listening carefully we learn that Turandot, in an effort to get her own back, has decreed that, until the Stranger's name is discovered, none shall sleep tonight. Calaf takes up this theme in his aria *Nessun dorma*. Although Puccini marked the opening phrases to be sung *pianissimo* they are usually belted out by tenors at such full blast that it is guaranteed that 'none shall sleep tonight'.

Our table-tennis team of Ping, Pong and Pang returns to try and persuade Calaf to reveal his name but in vain. They offer him gold: he refuses; they offer him jewels: he refuses; they offer him girls: he refuses. Shouting is heard and guards drag in Timur and Loo, who were seen talking to Calaf the previous evening. On Turandot's orders Loo is tortured but refuses to talk. No longer able to bear the pain she snatches a dagger from a guard and stabs herself. Her body is carried away, the crowds disperse and the bride-elect and her groom are left alone.

Tearing the veil from her face Calaf kisses her passionately. Instantly her iciness melts and she eagerly asks for more (aria: I was never kissed before in that kind of way). In an excessively overlong duet – by the time it's finished dawn has broken – Turandot confesses that she has loved Calaf all along and was only playing hard-to-get. He then reveals his name, the dawn brightens but – don't go home yet: there's another brief scene to come...

*Scene 2. Back to Square One.*
The final tableau shows Altoum and Co. seated in the palace, surrounded by as many supers as the management can afford. Calaf and Turandot enter, he smiling, she radiant, now transformed from an ice cold princess to a hot chick. Approaching the emperor, she announces she now knows the Stranger's name : it is...Love. Being a common surname, as proved by consulting the local telephone directory, no one is much the wiser, and with this corny ending the opera comes to a close. The rumbling noise heard at the end is the composer turning in his grave after listening to the finale he didn't compose.

# Werther

Opera in 4 acts by Jules Massenet.
First produced Vienna 1892

Werther, a poet                                  tenor

Albert, a villager                               baritone

Magistrate                                       bass

Charlotte, his daughter                          mezzo

Scene: Frankfurt                                 Time: 1780

Werther was a minor poet
an asthmatic, steeped in Fate
deep in love was he with Charlotte
daughter of a magistrate

He and Charlotte digged the fashion
reading Ossian's rhyme and verse
friendship ripened into passion
Werther's asthma just got worse

Albert was a handsome seeker
of fair Charlotte's dainty hand
Life for Werther then got bleaker
Bert was wealthy and had land

Sometimes Charlotte used to utter
to herself if things went wrong
"Keep on cutting bread and butter
it will make the children strong"

Werther, trying to forget her
was by foreign lands enticed
on returning home that winter
found that she and Bert were spliced

Lonely, saddened and dejected
Werther's sorrows knew no bound
as in life was he rejected
so in death his solace found

When his asthma just got worser
borrowed he a pistol, *ja!*
and began to sing the verses
of *Ah! non mi ridestar*

Werther pulled the fatal trigger
*bang!* the shot was like a mine
said the doctor on his rigor
mortis: "Hmm, he died at nine!"

Charlotte heard the news and uttered
"Life with him could never be,
now at last the bread is buttered
children, come inside for tea!"

Thus did end the life of Werther
by his own hand, there's the rub
but the novel, writ by Goethe
is still read on *Writers' Club!*

# William Tell

Opera in 4 acts by Gioacchino Rossini.
First produced Paris 1829

Principal characters

| | |
|---|---|
| William Tell, Swiss patriot | baritone |
| Jemmy, his son | soprano |
| Melchtal, village patriarch | bass |
| Arnold, his son | tenor |
| Mathilde, a Hapsburg princess | soprano |
| Gessler, Austrian governor | bass |

Scene: Switzerland            Time: 13$^{th}$ century

*Act 1. A village on the shores of Lake Lucerne. A triple wedding is being celebrated. A fisherman sings to the assembled population.*

Fisherman    This fish I bring thee's lost in contemplation
                this song I sing thee's lost in Swiss translation
                but when we've gained our self determination
                it's *schnapps* all round, a week of celebration!

*Melchtal blesses the happy couples. Tell and Arnold enter.*

Tell           We look to men like you for strength and honour
               Helvetia's hour of greatness is upon her
               Cruel Gessler's reign of terror must be ended
               our freedom must be won, our shores defended

*Leuthold, an old herdsman, rushes in, pursued by soldiers.*
Leut    *[to Tell]*  I need thy help to get me out of trouble
               these Gessler soldiers chase me at the double
               I killed one 'cause he tried to rape my daughter
               here's half a franc, get me across the water!

*Tell ferries the boat through the dangerous rapids and Leuthold to safety. The soldiers, finding Leuthold gone, loot the village and take old Melchtal hostage.*

*Act 2. A valley in the mountains. Mathilde is preparing a picnic for Arnold, who enters.*

Mat		I've climbed the highest mountain, what a view
		I've brought some *ementaler* for *fondue*
		for you a pair of *Schüblig* and some *rösti*
		some apple juice and vino if we're thirsty!

*Mathilde leaves. Arnold learns from Tell that his father has been murdered by Kessler's men. Arnold vows revenge and asks to join Tell's men. Patriots from surrounding cantons enter and swear allegiance to Tell.*
Tell		Today our country's future shall we bind
		the pact made with our brothers now is signed
		The day has dawned, long live the folk of Uri
		on Gessler's men we shall descend with fury!

*Act 3. The main square in Altdorf. It has been decreed that the population must pay homage to Gessler by bowing down to his hat displayed on a pole. Tell refuses.*

Gessler		To disobey my orders is a crime
		henceforth your life's not even worth a dime!
		your punishment for flouting what's been read
		is shoot an apple off your youngster's head!

*The villagers protest but are silenced by Gessler's soldiers. Tell turns to Jemmy.*
Tell		The apple that is placed upon thy head
		will split in two when fast my arrow's sped
		now here's thy test for courage and endurance *[aside]*
		if I should miss I'll claim from "*Swiss Insurance!*"

*Tell successfully shoots the apple from Jemmy's head. He tells Gessler that a second arrow was for him had he missed the first time. Enraged, Gessler condemns Tell and Jemmy to death but Mathilde intervenes and asks that Jemmy be handed over to her.*

Mat *[to Gessler]*	Your cruelty's beyond all comprehension
		henceforth will Jemmy be in my protection
		your action is in direct contravention
		of protocol and Geneva Convention!
*Mathilde takes Jemmy under her protection but Tell is arrested and taken to prison.*

*Act 4. Scene 1. Arnold visits his father's home, burnt down by Gessler's men.*

Arnold          Unhappy home! This house where I was born
                    burnt to the ground, its cinders make me mourn
                    'tis well my father sawest not this dreadful sight
                    these blackened walls would make him die of fright!

*[looks around]*

                    But father, I remember, had a mission
                    he in this house hid arms and ammunition
                    so while these fumes of burning timber waft
                    I'll take a butcher's hook up in the loft!

*Arnold discovers a secret cache of weapons. As his men arm themselves news arrives that Tell has been taken prisoner. They vow to rescue Tell and start the revolt.*

Chorus          We'll crush the foe, their blood will flow
                    their pleading is in vain
                    Tell with his bow will strike the blow
                    Our Swiss Rolls on again!

*Scene 2. The shores of Lake Lucerne. A storm is breaking. Jemmy lights a beacon, the signal for the revolt to begin. Tell, freed by his captors, steers his boat to the shore and having regained his crossbow slays Gessler. As the storm subsides the people give thanks for their liberation.*

Tell              The hated tyrant Gessler is no more
                    the people may rejoice, both rich and poor
                    Helvetia has thrown off its foreign yoke

*[to Jemmy sotto voce]*
                    I'm feeling rather parched, grab me a coke!

All               Let all rejoice, the enemy's surrendered
                    the Swiss have won, the struggle is now ended
                    our fields and pastures will return so lush
                    our cows will dance Rossini's *ranz des vaches!*

                    This opera at long last is now replete
                    its four long acts are over and complete
                    let's all get home, our appetites to quell
                    and let us pray that one day time *Will Tell!*

ENDS

Music and Books published by Travis & Emery Music Bookshop:

Anon.: Hymnarium Sarisburiense, cum Rubricis et Notis Musicis.
Anon.: Säcularfeier des Geburtstages von Ludwig van Beethoven
Agricola, Johann Friedrich from Tosi: Anleitung zur Singkunst.
Bach, C.P.E.: edited W. Emery: Nekrolog or Obituary Notice of J.S. Bach.
Bateson, Naomi Judith: Alcock of Salisbury
Bathe, William: A Briefe Introduction to the Skill of Song
Bax, Arnold: Symphony #5, Arranged for Piano Four Hands by Walter Emery
Burney, Charles: The Present State of Music in France and Italy
Burney, Charles: The Present State of Music in Germany, The Netherlands ...
Burney, Charles: An Account of the Musical Performances ... Handel
Burney, Karl: Nachricht von Georg Friedrich Handel's Lebensumstanden.
Burns, Robert: The Caledonian Musical Museum ..The Best Scotch Songs. (1810)
Cobbett, W.W.: Cobbett's Cyclopedic Survey of Chamber Music. (2 vols.)
Corrette, Michel: Le Maitre de Clavecin
Crimp, Bryan: Dear Mr. Rosenthal ... Dear Mr. Gaisberg ...
Crimp, Bryan: Solo: The Biography of Solomon
Crotch, William: Substance of Several Courses of Lectures on Music
d'Indy, Vincent: Beethoven: Biographie Critique
d'Indy, Vincent: Beethoven: A Critical Biography
d'Indy, Vincent: César Franck (in French)
Fischhof, Joseph: Versuch einer Geschichte des Clavierbaues. (Faksimile 1853).
Frescobaldi, Girolamo: D'Arie Musicali per Cantarsi. Primo & Secondo Libro.
Geminiani, Francesco: The Art of Playing the Violin.
Handel; Purcell; Boyce; Geene et al: Calliope or English Harmony: Volume First.
Häuser: Musikalisches Lexikon. 2 vols in one.
Hawkins, John: A General History of the Science and Practice of Music (5 vols.)
Herbert-Caesari, Edgar: The Science and Sensations of Vocal Tone
Herbert-Caesari, Edgar: Vocal Truth
Hopkins and Rimboult: The Organ. Its History and Construction.
Hunt, John: - see separate list of discographies at the end of these titles
Isaacs, Lewis: Hänsel and Gretel. A Guide to Humperdinck's Opera.
Isaacs, Lewis: Königskinder (Royal Children) A Guide to Humperdinck's Opera.
Kastner: Manuel Général de Musique Militaire
Lacassagne, M. l'Abbé Joseph :  Traité Général des élémens du Chant.
Lascelles (née Catley), Anne: The Life of Miss Anne Catley.
Mainwaring, John: Memoirs of the Life of the Late George Frederic Handel
Malcolm, Alexander: A Treaty of Music: Speculative, Practical and Historical
Marx, Adolph Bernhard: Die Kunst des Gesanges, Theoretisch-Practisch
May, Florence:  The Life of Brahms
May, Florence:  The Girlhood Of Clara Schumann: Clara Wieck And Her Time.
Mellers, Wilfrid: Angels of the Night: Popular Female Singers of Our Time
Mellers, Wilfrid: Bach and the Dance of God
Mellers, Wilfrid: Beethoven and the Voice of God
Mellers, Wilfrid: Caliban Reborn - Renewal in Twentieth Century Music
Mellers, Wilfrid: Darker Shade of Pale, A Backdrop to Bob DylanMellers, Wilfrid: François Couperin and the French Classical Tradition
Mellers, Wilfrid: Harmonious Meeting
Mellers, Wilfrid: Le Jardin Retrouvé, The Music of Frederic Mompou

Mellers, Wilfrid: Music and Society, England and the European Tradition
Mellers, Wilfrid: Music in a New Found Land: ... ... American Music
Mellers, Wilfrid: Romanticism and the Twentieth Century (from 1800)
Mellers, Wilfrid: The Masks of Orpheus: ...... the Story of European Music.
Mellers, Wilfrid: The Sonata Principle (from c. 1750)
Mellers, Wilfrid: Vaughan Williams and the Vision of Albion
Panchianio, Cattuffio: Rutzvanscad II Giovine
Pearce, Charles: Sims Reeves, Fifty Years of Music in England.
Playford, John: An Introduction to the Skill of Musick.
Purcell, Henry et al: Harmonia Sacra ... The First Book, (1726)
Purcell, Henry et al: Harmonia Sacra ... Book II (1726)
Quantz, Johann: Versuch einer Anweisung die Flöte trave      rsiere zu spielen.
Rameau, Jean-Philippe: Code de Musique Pratique, ou Methodes.
Rameau, Jean-Philippe: Erreurs sur La Musique dans l'Encyclopédie
Rastall, Richard: The Notation of Western Music.
Rimbault, Edward: The Pianoforte, Its Origins, Progress, and Construction.
Rousseau, Jean Jacques: Dictionnaire de Musique
Rubinstein, Anton : Guide to the proper use of the Pianoforte Pedals.
Sainsbury, John S.: Dictionary of Musicians. (1825). 2 vols.
Serré de Rieux, Jean de : Les dons des Enfans de Latone
Simpson, Christopher: A Compendium of Practical Musick in Five Parts
Spohr, Louis: Autobiography
Spohr, Louis: Grand Violin School
Tans'ur, William: A New Musical Grammar; or The Harmonical Spectator
Terry, Charles Sanford: Bach's Chorals – Parts 1, 2 and 3.
Terry, Charles Sanford: John Christian Bach
Terry, Charles Sanford: J.S. Bach's Original Hymn-Tunes for Congregational Use.
Terry, Charles Sanford: Four-Part Chorals of J.S. Bach. (German & English)
Terry, Charles Sanford: Joh. Seb. Bach, Cantata Texts, Sacred and Secular.
Terry, Charles Sanford: The Origins of the Family of Bach Musicians.
Tosi, Pierfrancesco: Opinioni de' Cantori Antichi, e Moderni
Tosi, Pierfrancesco: Observations on the Florid Song.
Van der Straeten, Edmund: History of the Violoncello, The Viol da Gamba ...
Van der Straeten, Edmund: History of the Violin, Its Ancestors... (2 vols.)
Walther, J. G. [Waltern]: Musicalisches Lexikon [Musikalisches Lexicon]
Wagner, Richard: Beethoven (Leipzig 1870)
Wagner, Richard: Lebens-Bericht (Leipzig 1884)
Wagner, Richard: The Musaic of the Future (Translated by E. Dannreuther).
Zwirn, Gerald: Stranded Stories From The Operas

Travis & Emery Music Bookshop
17 Cecil Court, London, WC2N 4EZ, United Kingdom.
Tel. (+44) 20 7240 2129
© Travis & Emery 2010

Discographies by Travis & Emery:

Discographies by John Hunt.

1987: From Adam to Webern: the Recordings of von Karajan.
1991: 3 Italian Conductors and 7 Viennese Sopranos: 10 Discographies: Arturo Toscanini, Guido Cantelli, Carlo Maria Giulini, Elisabeth Schwarzkopf, Irmgard Seefried, Elisabeth Gruemmer, Sena Jurinac, Hilde Gueden, Lisa Della Casa, Rita Streich.
1992: Mid-Century Conductors and More Viennese Singers: 10 Discographies: Karl Boehm, Victor De Sabata, Hans Knappertsbusch, Tullio Serafin, Clemens Krauss, Anton Dermota, Leonie Rysanek, Eberhard Waechter, Maria Reining, Erich Kunz.
1993: More 20th Century Conductors: 7 Discographies: Eugen Jochum, Ferenc Fricsay, Carl Schuricht, Felix Weingartner, Josef Krips, Otto Klemperer, Erich Kleiber.
1994: Giants of the Keyboard: 6 Discographies: Wilhelm Kempff, Walter Gieseking, Edwin Fischer, Clara Haskil, Wilhelm Backhaus, Artur Schnabel.
1994: Six Wagnerian Sopranos: 6 Discographies: Frieda Leider, Kirsten Flagstad, Astrid Varnay, Martha Moedl, Birgit Nilsson, Gwyneth Jones.
1995: Musical Knights: 6 Discographies: Henry Wood, Thomas Beecham, Adrian Boult, John Barbirolli, Reginald Goodall, Malcolm Sargent.
1995: A Notable Quartet: 4 Discographies: Gundula Janowitz, Christa Ludwig, Nicolai Gedda, Dietrich Fischer-Dieskau.
1996: 978-0-952582-75-5: Leopold Stokowski (1882-1977): Discography and Concert Register
1996: Makers of the Philharmonia: 11 Discographies: Alceo Galliera, Walter Susskind, Paul Kletzki, Nicolai Malko, Issay Dobrowen, Lovro Von Matacic, Efrem Kurtz, Otto Ackermann, Anatole Fistoulari, George Weldon, Robert Irving.
1996: The Post-War German Tradition: 5 Discographies: Rudolf Kempe, Joseph Keilberth, Wolfgang Sawallisch, Rafael Kubelik, Andre Cluytens.
1996: Teachers and Pupils: 7 Discographies: Elisabeth Schwarzkopf, Maria Ivoguen, Maria Cebotari, Meta Seinemeyer, Ljuba Welitsch, Rita Streich, Erna Berger.
1996: Leopold Stokowski: Discography and Concert Listing.
1996: Makers of the Philharmonia: 11 Discographies Alceo Galliera, Walter Susskind, Paul Kletzki, Nicolai Malko, Issay Dobrowen, Lovro Von Matacic, Efrem Kurtz, Otto Ackermann, Anatole Fistoulari, George Weldon, Robert Irving.
1996: Tenors in a Lyric Tradition: 3 Discographies: Peter Anders, Walther Ludwig, Fritz Wunderlich.
1997: The Lyric Baritone: 5 Discographies: Hans Reinmar, Gerhard Huesch, Josef Metternich, Hermann Uhde, Eberhard Waechter.
1997: Hungarians in Exile: 3 Discographies: Fritz Reiner, Antal Dorati, George Szell.
1997: The Art of the Diva: 3 Discographies: Claudia Muzio, Maria Callas, Magda Olivero.
1997: Metropolitan Sopranos: 4 Discographies: Rosa Ponselle, Eleanor Steber, Zinka Milanov, Leontyne Price.
1997: Back From The Shadows: 4 Discographies: Willem Mengelberg, Dimitri Mitropoulos, Hermann Abendroth, Eduard Van Beinum.
1997: More Musical Knights: 4 Discographies: Hamilton Harty, Charles Mackerras, Simon Rattle, John Pritchard.
1998: More Giants of the Keyboard: 5 Discographies: Claudio Arrau, Gyorgy Cziffra, Vladimir Horowitz, Dinu Lipatti, Artur Rubinstein.

1998: Conductors On The Yellow Label: 8 Discographies: Fritz Lehmann, Ferdinand Leitner, Ferenc Fricsay, Eugen Jochum, Leopold Ludwig, Artur Rother, Franz Konwitschny, Igor Markevitch.
1998: Mezzo and Contraltos: 5 Discographies: Janet Baker, Margarete Klose, Kathleen Ferrier, Giulietta Simionato, Elisabeth Hoengen.
1999: The Furtwaengler Sound Sixth Edition: Discography and Concert Listing.
1999: The Great Dictators: 3 Discographies: Evgeny Mravinsky, Artur Rodzinski, Sergiu Celibidache.
1999: Sviatoslav Richter: Pianist of the Century: Discography.
2000: Philharmonic Autocrat 1: Discography of: Herbert Von Karajan [Third Edition].
2000: Wiener Philharmoniker 1 - Vienna Philharmonic and Vienna State Opera Orchestras: Discography Part 1 1905-1954.
2000: Wiener Philharmoniker 2 - Vienna Philharmonic and Vienna State Opera Orchestras: Discography Part 2 1954-1989.
2001: Gramophone Stalwarts: 3 Separate Discographies: Bruno Walter, Erich Leinsdorf, Georg Solti.
2001: Singers of the Third Reich: 5 Discographies: Helge Roswaenge, Tiana Lemnitz, Franz Voelker, Maria Mueller, Max Lorenz.
2001: Philharmonic Autocrat 2: Concert Register of Herbert Von Karajan Second Edition.
2002: Sächsische Staatskapelle Dresden: Complete Discography.
2002: Carlo Maria Giulini: Discography and Concert Register.
2002: Pianists For The Connoisseur: 6 Discographies: Arturo Benedetti Michelangeli, Alfred Cortot, Alexis Weissenberg, Clifford Curzon, Solomon, Elly Ney.
2003: Singers on the Yellow Label: 7 Discographies: Maria Stader, Elfriede Troetschel, Annelies Kupper, Wolfgang Windgassen, Ernst Haefliger, Josef Greindl, Kim Borg.
2003: A Gallic Trio: 3 Discographies: Charles Muench, Paul Paray, Pierre Monteux.
2004: Antal Dorati 1906-1988: Discography and Concert Register.
2004: Columbia 33CX Label Discography.
2004: Great Violinists: 3 Discographies: David Oistrakh, Wolfgang Schneiderhan, Arthur Grumiaux.
2006: Leopold Stokowski: Second Edition of the Discography.
2006: Wagner Im Festspielhaus: Discography of the Bayreuth Festival.
2006: Her Master's Voice: Concert Register and Discography of Dame Elisabeth Schwarzkopf [Third Edition].
2007: Hans Knappertsbusch: Kna: Concert Register and Discography of Hans Knappertsbusch, 1888-1965. Second Edition.
2008: Philips Minigroove: Second Extended Version of the European Discography.
2009: American Classics: The Discographies of Leonard Bernstein and Eugene Ormandy.
2010: Dirigenten der DDR: Conductors of the German Democratic Republic

Discography by Stephen J. Pettitt, edited by John Hunt:
1987: 978-1-906857-16-5: Philharmonia Orchestra: Complete Discography 1945-1987

Available from: Travis & Emery at 17 Cecil Court, London, UK.
(+44) 20 7 240 2129. email on sales@travis-and-emery.com .

© Travis & Emery 2010

www.ingramcontent.com/pod-product-compliance
Lightning Source LLC
Chambersburg PA
CBHW061304110426
42742CB00012BA/2054